EVENTS THAT
CHANGED THE
WORLD

1800–1820

The Nineteenth Century

**Other books in the
Events That Changed the World series:**

EVENTS THAT
CHANGED THE
WORLD

1800–1820
=The Nineteenth Century=

Jodie L. Zdrok, *Book Editor*

Bruce Glassman, *Vice President*
Bonnie Szumski, *Publisher*
Helen Cothran, *Managing Editor*

GREENHAVEN PRESS
An imprint of Thomson Gale, a part of The Thomson Corporation

THOMSON
———✦———™
GALE

Detroit • New York • San Francisco • San Diego • New Haven, Conn.
Waterville, Maine • London • Munich

For more information, contact
Greenhaven Press
27500 Drake Rd.
Farmington Hills, MI 48331-3535
Or you can visit our Internet site at http://www.gale.com

LIBRARY OF CONGRESS CATALOGING-IN-PUBLICATION DATA
1800–1820 : the nineteenth century / Jodie L. Zdrok, book editor.
p. cm. — (Events that changed the world)
Includes bibliographical references and index.
ISBN 0-7377-2029-8 (lib. : alk. paper)
1. History, Modern—19th century. 2. Civilization, Modern—19th century.
I. Zdrok, Jodie L. II. Series.
D358.A124 2005
909.81—dc22   2004052322

Printed in the United States of America

CONTENTS

Event 9: The Brothers Grimm Publish a Fairy-Tale Collection: 1812

Event 10: The Congress of Vienna Ends Napoléon's Empire: October 1, 1814

Event 11: Napoléon's Final Defeat Takes Place at the Battle of Waterloo: June 18, 1815

Event 12: Repatriated Slaves Sail for Liberia: February 6, 1820

Event 13: Percy Bysshe Shelley Publishes *Prometheus Unbound:* Summer 1820

FOREWORD

I n 1543 a Polish astronomer named Nicolaus Copernicus published a book entitled *De revolutionibus orbium coelestium* in which he theorized that Earth revolved around the Sun. In 1688, during the Glorious Revolution, Dutch prince William of Orange invaded England and overthrew King James II. In 1922 Irish author James Joyce's novel *Ulysses*, which describes one day in Dublin, was published.

Although these events are seemingly unrelated, occurring in different nations and in different centuries, they all share the distinction of having changed the world. Although Copernicus's book had a relatively minor impact at the time of its publication, it eventually had a momentous influence. The Copernican system provided a foundation on which future scientists could develop an accurate understanding of the solar system. Perhaps more importantly, it required humanity to contemplate the possibility that Earth, far from occupying a special place at the center of creation, was merely one planet in a vast universe. In doing so, it forced a reevaluation of the Christian cosmology that had served as the foundation of Western culture. As professor Thomas S. Kuhn writes, "The drama of Christian life and the morality that had been made dependent upon it would not readily adapt to a universe in which the earth was just one of a number of planets."

Like the Copernican revolution, the Glorious Revolution of 1688–1689 had a profound influence on the future of Western societies. By deposing James II, William and his wife, Mary, ended the Stuart dynasty, a series of monarchs who had favored the Catholic Church and had limited the power of Parliament for decades. Under William and Mary, Parliament passed the Bill of Rights, which established the legislative supremacy of Parliament and barred Roman Catholics from the throne. These actions initiated the gradual process by which the power of the government of England shifted from the monarchy to Parliament, establishing a democratic system that would be copied, with some variations, by the United States and other democratic societies worldwide.

Whereas the Glorious Revolution had a major impact in the political sphere, the publication of Joyce's novel *Ulysses* represented
a revolution in literature. In an effort to capture the sense of chaos
and discontinuity that permeated the culture in the wake of World
War I, Joyce did away with the use of straightforward narrative
that had dominated fiction up to that time. The novel, whose structure mirrors that of Homer's *Odyssey*, combines realistic descriptions of events with passages that convey the characters' inner experience by means of a technique known as stream of
consciousness, in which the characters' thoughts and feelings are
presented without regard to logic or narrative order. Due to its departure from the traditional modes of fiction, *Ulysses* is often described as one of the seminal works of modernist literature. As
stated by Pennsylvania State University professor Michael H. Beg-
nal, "*Ulysses* is the novel that changed the direction of 20th-cen-
tury fiction written in English."

Copernicus's theory of a sun-centered solar system, the Glorious Revolution, and James Joyce's *Ulysses* are just three examples of time-bound events that have had far-reaching effects—for
better or worse—on the progress of human societies worldwide.
History is made up of an inexhaustible list of such events. In the
twentieth century alone, for example, one can isolate any number
of world-shattering moments: the first performance of Igor
Stravinsky's ballet *The Rites of Spring* in 1913; Japan's attack on
Pearl Harbor on December 7, 1941; the launch of the satellite
Sputnik on October 4, 1957. These events variously influenced the
culture, society, and political configuration of the twentieth century.

Greenhaven Press's Events That Changed the World series is
designed to help readers learn about world history by examining
seemingly random events that have had the greatest influence on
the development of cultures, societies, and governments throughout the ages. The series is divided into sets of several anthologies,
with each set covering a period of one hundred years. Each volume begins with an introduction that provides essential context on
the time period being covered. Then, the major events of the era
are covered by means of primary and secondary sources. Primary
sources include firsthand accounts, speeches, correspondence, and
other materials that bring history alive. Secondary sources analyze
the profound effects the events had on the world. Each reading is
preceded by an introduction that puts it in context and emphasizes

the event's importance in the ongoing evolution of world history. Additional features add to the value of the series: An annotated table of contents and an index allow readers to quickly locate material of interest. A chronology provides an easy reference for contextual information. And a bibliography offers opportunities for further exploration. All of these features help to make the Events That Changed the World series a valuable resource for readers interested in the major events that have shaped the course of humanity.

INTRODUCTION

The early nineteenth century was dominated by a single man: Napoléon Bonaparte, emperor of France. The greatest military leader of modern times, Napoléon was a brilliant tactician and superb administrator who amassed one of the largest empires in history in a mere twelve years. He was also a ruthless dictator, a brazen nepotist, and ultimately a megalomaniac whose fall was as precipitous as his rise. His influence on the political, geographical, and cultural history of Europe and the Americas is so significant that the period from 1796 to 1815 is known as the Napoleonic era.

Napoléon was not French by birth. In 1769 he was born Napoleone Buonaparte to a family of Italian origin in Corsica. He was educated at military schools in France and rose quickly through the ranks of French artillery regiments during the French Revolution. The Directory, France's postrevolutionary government, put him in command of military campaigns that conquered large territories in Italy and Egypt between 1796 and 1799. The popular general then toppled the Directory in a 1799 coup d'état, accepted the title of consul for life in 1802, and proclaimed himself emperor (and his empire hereditary) in 1804.

Napoléon sold France's vast Louisiana Territory to the United States in 1803, abandoning his dream of an overseas empire. Instead he focused his energies on conquest of Europe by invasion, annexation, and treaty, and on economic strangulation of England by trade embargoes when British naval superiority made military invasion impossible. According to historian Anthony Halperin:

> By 1810 to 1811, Napoleon's empire included nearly all of Europe except for the Balkans. It was comprised of an enlarged France (which had swallowed Belgium and Holland, parts of Germany, and the Italian coast all the way to Rome) and various puppet nations actually ruled by Napoleon or by a Bonaparte subservient to Napoleon. In addition to those lands he ruled over directly, Napoleon held alliances with Austria, Russia, Denmark, Sweden, and a greatly reduced Prussia. Essentially all of Europe was now

"at war" with Britain, their resources and industry and populations being used to serve the French Empire.[1]

Numerous coalitions of European powers tried unsuccessfully to halt Napoléon's advances, with far-reaching consequences. For example, while major colonial powers Spain and Portugal were preoccupied with the Napoleonic Wars, they lost control of their colonies in Central and South America, where independence movements embraced Napoléon's antimonarchy, nationalistic fervor.

Napoléon the General: Military Reforms

As he expanded and consolidated his empire, Napoléon effected military reforms that led to the modern army and modern warfare. First, according to biographer Ida M. Tarbell, "War was no longer left to the professionals; the day of the citizen soldier had arrived. To raise its armies, the French used conscription [i.e., the draft; mandatory rather than voluntary service], a practice that soon was to spread to the rest of Europe."[2]

With a ready supply of soldiers, Napoléon combined infantry, artillery, and cavalry units into larger and larger divisions, then sent them into battle with simple, direct strategies that seem obvious today but were innovative at the time: Fight on favorable terrain and move quickly. Attack the enemy at its weakest point. Breach enemy lines, then outflank them. Disrupt the enemy's battle plans. With such tactics he overpowered opposing armies for nearly twenty years.

Napoléon the Administrator: Social and Legal Reforms

Napoléon also embarked on an ambitious program of government reorganization and social reforms. He built many secondary and technical schools and put the educational system, including university curricula and teacher training, under the control of the central government. He standardized weights and measures and imposed the metric system throughout the empire. (The metric system took hold, but Napoléon's new calendar, with months of three ten-day weeks, did not.)

In line with revolutionary principles of equality, Napoléon created a new order of merit for which any man or woman was eligible, the Legion of Honor, which remains France's highest civilian honor. Many historians consider his highest achievement to be his reform of the French legal system. Prior to his rule, France had no single code of laws. The Napoleonic Code of 1804 instituted a uniform civil law code also in keeping with egalitarian principles. According to Halperin, Napoléon "did not believe that every country was a special situation that deserved unique treatment":

> Instead, he was a "universalist," believing that the same universal truths and laws applied exactly the same, everywhere. He therefore spread his system of laws, the Napoleonic Code, to all of the territories he controlled, with only minor changes from place to place. Although Napoleon brought conflict wherever he went, he also spread the idea of societies in which everyone was equal before the law, and where legal privileges for certain classes did not exist. Napoleon did what he could to end peasantry, although in Eastern Europe . . . peasantry seemed to continue even when it was legally outlawed, because the same people continued to own the land, and the same people continued to work it. In general, though, the Napoleonic Code was a dramatically modernizing force, bringing about social reform from its effects on modernizing of the Prussian bureaucracy into a meritocracy to its creation of the idea of the totally secular state.[3]

Public and Personal Contradictions

Among the contradictions that have fascinated historians and biographers since Napoléon's day is the contrast between the democratic, liberal ideals reflected in his Napoleonic Code and his authoritarian political practices. He believed in liberty, equality, fraternity—the goals of the revolution—and a man's right to succeed through talent and ability without distinctions of birth, just as he had risen from obscurity. But he essentially replaced the old aristocracy with a new one made up of his own large family, as Halperin points out:

> Napoleon [appointed his seven] brothers and sisters as royalty throughout Europe. When he ran out of family, he switched to more distant relatives and the servants he believed most faithful. For instance, when Napoleon had to transfer his brother Joseph from Naples to rule over Spain, he made one of his leading generals, Murat [who was, not coincidentally, also his brother-in-law], into the King of Naples. He also made his stepson . . . into the viceroy of the Kingdom of Italy.[4]

The dictator also crushed opposition with a network of secret police and spies and strictly censored the press, reducing the number of newspapers in Paris from sixty in 1799 to four in 1814.

Throughout his rule he promoted scientific research and public education, but only within limits. Historian-filmmaker David Grubin explains:

> After conquering Egypt, he founded the Institut d'Égypte, through which mathematicians, mapmakers, and engineers studied mummies, surveyed temples and discovered the Rosetta Stone, which proved to be the key to deciphering Egyptian hieroglyphics. "The true conquests," Bonaparte wrote, "the only ones that leave no regret, are those that have been wrested from ignorance." But it was Bonaparte alone who would later dictate what knowledge was permissible. "Education," he said, "must impart the same knowledge and the same principles to all individuals living in the same society, in order to create a single, uniform body, informed with one and the same understanding, and working for the common good on the basis of uniformity of views."[5]

Napoléon prized architecture and commissioned such works as the monumental Arc de Triomphe. He patronized the arts in general, including the new artistic movement known as Romanticism, which represented emotion, imagination, nationalistic greatness, and heroic individualism. But he plundered the artistic riches of Egypt and other conquered territories to enrich Paris, and he alienated as well as inspired great artists. German composer Ludwig van Beethoven, for example, at first revered Napoléon as the embodiment of the ideals of the French Revolution, but Beethoven is said to have been so infuriated and disillusioned by Napoléon's self-elevation to emperor in 1804 that he tore up the dedication of his new Third Symphony, originally titled *Bonaparte*, and published it as *Eroica* instead.

In some ways Napoléon was the victim of historical irony. Always a shrewd propagandist—he commissioned artwork glorifying himself in larger-than-life imagery and created his own newspapers glorifying his military victories—his efforts appear to have backfired. Halperin notes that counterpropaganda provoked by Napoléon's self-promotion provided lasting images of the man as "a diminutive brat [that erased] Napoleon's self-constructed imperial image as a powerful god-like ruler. . . . To this day Napoleon's imperial image is popularly conflated with his satirical representation—namely his short stature, which is largely a satiric invention."[6]

Sudden Downfall, Enduring Legacy

Also ironically, his great military strengths led to his defeat. Napoléon's downfall began with his famous failed invasion of Russia and disastrous retreat from Moscow in 1812. Napoléon restored his armies' strength in numbers with conscription, but though he remained a formidable military commander, his forces were overwhelmed by a new coalition and he was forced into exile in Elba in 1814. He returned to France and attempted to regain power in March 1815 at the head of new armies in a daring attack known as the Hundred Days, but he was finally defeated by the Duke of Wellington at Waterloo, in one of the great battles of history, largely because the armies of the British and the Prussians used some of his own innovative tactics against him.

Ultimately, control of his empire depended on winning battles; once Napoléon's armies were soundly defeated, so was he. The allies banished Napoléon again, this time to the barren island of St. Helena, where he spent the remaining six years of his life writing his memoirs while a two-thousand-man guard made sure this exile was permanent.

Few empires formed by military conquest and held together by tyrannical force long outlive the reign of their founders. Napoléon's empire was no exception. Nonetheless, Napoléon shaped history largely because he established institutions and fostered ideals that endured long after he and his empire vanished.

In 1815, Europeans and their far-flung former colonies were left to figure out what form of government should replace Napoleonic rule; how to redraw maps and reestablish national identities, political alliances, and trade; and what directions the scientific and academic inquiry he promoted would take. Over the following decades, most struggled to do so according to Napoléon's modern worldview and the movements he epitomized: nationalism, secularism, and Romantic individualism. Greenhaven's *Events That Changed the World: 1800–1820* examines the significant events and developments of the Napoleonic era to help readers understand not only their immediate effects but also their profound historical consequences.

Notes

1. Anthony Halperin, "Napoleon's Vast Empire: 1809–1811," *Napoleonic Satires*, 2003. Brown University Library Digital Collection. http://dl.lib. brown.edu/napoleon/timeline.html.

2. Ida M. Tarbell, *A Life of Napoleon Bonaparte.* New York and London: McClure, Phillips, 1901. http://ragz-international.com/french_revolution_ and_napoleon.htm.

3. Halperin, "Napoleon's Vast Empire."

4. Halperin, "Napoleon's Vast Empire."

5. David Grubin, "Tyrant or Hero," *Napoleon: The Man and the Myth*, PBS, November 2000. www.pbs.org.

6. Halperin, "Napoleon's Vast Empire."

The Act of Union Resulted in Conflict Between Britain and Ireland

by Patrick O'Farrell

The United Kingdom formally came into existence on January 1, 1801, when the Act of Union officially made Ireland a part of Great Britain. British prime minister William Pitt and his Irish chief secretary Lord Castlereagh decided that religious conflicts in Ireland could be better handled if Ireland was united with the rest of Great Britain, which included England, Scotland, and Wales. The union of Great Britain and Ireland provided a newfound legal equality between the Irish Catholic majority and the Irish Protestant minority because both were now represented equally in a single parliament under the United Kingdom.

This union was unpopular with many Irish citizens. Despite the intentions of Pitt and Castlereagh, religious conflict among the Irish continued. In addition, British-Irish relations deteriorated in the years following the union. As Patrick O'Farrell indicates in the following article, mutual misconceptions—of the English as oppressors and of the Irish as unruly—affected the course of the British-Irish relationship. The author notes that differences between British interests and Irish goals fueled the sentiment. O'Farrell reminds us that the bitterness that emerged after the 1801 union remains entrenched to the present day.

Australian historian Patrick O'Farrell of the University of South Wales is the author of numerous books on history of the Catholic Church in Australia, the Irish in Australia, and Irish migration.

U nder the Union, as before, the relationship between England and Ireland was one of subjection, met by continued criticism and recurrent resistance. Immediately one seeks to expand or explain this simplicity, a tortuous maze of images obtrudes, images no less important than reality, dynamic images 'that yet/Fresh images beget.' All facets of the Anglo-Irish relationship were decisively influenced by powerful mental representations—presumptions, conceptions, impressions, understandings—to which reality was subordinated. Substantially it was a relationship conducted on the level of stereotypes and prejudices.

A Culture Clash

The Union of 1800 imported the relationship with Ireland into the centre of the British political system. Where before Ireland might be regarded as virtually foreign affairs, its political integration gave it direct domestic dimensions for Britain, and the persistent difficulties encountered in dealing with it compelled attention to explaining and understanding what was taking place and why.

The culture clash situation, as has been suggested, disposed the superior power both to exalt its own virtues, and to reject the subject culture as either not worth understanding, or as amply understood in negative and derogatory terms. This evaluation bred bitter resentment, and the impulse, within the subject culture, to both prove its own worth and to argue that what the conquerors saw as their own virtues were in reality vices. This abrasion was exacerbated by the factor of distance: the two cultures were close enough for constant friction, too distant to mingle easily.

Then there were the consequences of the preponderance of British power. A relationship in which superior power always remained an ultimate potential solvent did not elicit understanding as an imperative need: it could well be easier to simply discipline the Irish rather than to attempt to discover what agitated them. The availability to Britain of resort to coercion did much to vitiate and delay the development of understanding. It entrenched the view that the only treatment the Irish understood was coercion and convinced the Irish that the only policy of which Britain was capable was coercion. *The Times* laid it down in 1867: '. . . the Englishman's view of the question is that which must prevail in the end, whatever temporary and partial expedients may be applied.' If that was what the relationship must boil down to, in an English view, then it was on the field of force that the Irish must challenge it, if they were determined to do so.

The power of artificial, partial, and convenient depictions of reality was particularly great in a situation where experience of reality at firsthand was severely restricted by ignorance and unfamiliarity. Relatively few Englishmen knew Ireland other than indirectly, through what they read or were told: those who had visited Ireland tended to know it only in its Anglo-Irish aspect. In 1880, M.F. Cusack reported that he had found in England 'an extraordinary and almost total ignorance as to the true state of Irish affairs. I believe this arose partly from want of correct historical information and partly from a want of that personal knowledge of this country which could only be obtained by a residence in it. . . .' Cusack pointed to one illustration of the consequences of such ignorance when it was allied with the habitual presumption that what prevailed in England also existed in Ireland, and to a similar degree: 'English gentlemen naturally suppose that the Irish peasant, or small farmer, has the social advantages of the Englishman of his class, hence they cannot possibly understand one-half of the causes which contribute to make Ireland poor and discontented.' This mixture of ignorance and presumption might not have been so divisive and dangerous had the Irish recognized its existence, but they did not. Cusack remarked that the Irish patriot 'does not always give his English friends credit for their ignorance, nor probably . . . will he understand it.' Some of this ignorance was deliberate, in the sense that Englishmen, like any other people, were adept at avoiding the contemplation of unpleasantness and failure. But the Irish nationalist view, assuming knowledge where it did not exist, neglected education in favour of an aggressive berating, and saw malice where the reality was often ignorance and neglect.

The Power of Images

Once established, images had a coercive power, the power by which life may be compelled to imitate art. The expectation that events and people would conform to images of them sometimes produced precisely that result. Coercion of Irishmen deemed to be terrorists produced terrorists. The swing of Irish public opinion towards support of the 1916 rebellion is often attributed to the way in which England responded to it. It might also be attributed to a reaction against the English depiction of it. The English saw the rebellion as treachery in which all Ireland had conspired. All Ireland had not, but the English determination or willingness to cast Ireland in that role fostered a growing popular enactment of it.

Images bred acceptance of type-cast roles of mutual estrangement from which the actors could never escape: whatever the changes in the empirical situation, Paddys and terrorists would always confront imperialists and landlords because that was the way in which the participants conceived their conflict, thus dooming it to repeat itself in the old ways, and thus reviving all the traditional antipathies. So, the idealized and pure Britain revered by nineteenth-century Protestant Unionists no longer exists, if it ever did. And the Britain reviled by traditional Irish nationalists is changed also—as is the Pope's green island of Paddys [Irish people] and peasants. But these traditional images work still to prevent the emergence of present realities.

A basic problem has been that images derived from situations of conflict perpetuate both the conflict and themselves. The old images breed new conflict which, being interpreted in terms of those images, confirms and sustains them. New events are fed back into the historical continuum thus intensifying the influence both of contemporary events and of their historical precursors. Attempts by politicians to disown traditional images or allow them to become irrelevant are extremely hazardous, as this is seen as betrayal or weakness. Politicians were—and are—expected to live up to popular expectations based on images. In August 1969 Mr Jack Lynch, the Prime Minister of the Irish Republic, made moves and declarations in keeping with the mood of an electorate long fed on images of eventual desirable Irish unity: Mr Chichester Clark, Prime Minister of Northern Ireland, interpreted the disorder which had provoked Lynch's reaction, as a conspiracy of hooliganism manipulated by the Republic in a campaign for unity. Both politicians were aware of the unreality and inadequacy of the images to which they gave lip-service, but they were constrained by the power of tradition. The bigger and more obvious the gap between what really existed and what traditionalists believed ought to exist, the greater was the pressure from such traditionalists to make ideals into reality. The celebration in 1966 of the fiftieth anniversary of the Easter Rebellion drew attention to the distance which separated the Republic from the national ideals of 1916. Reforms in Northern Ireland were seen as departures from the ideal. In both cases, extremists had a firm image of what their ideal was: the question was, to what lengths would they go to achieve or preserve it?

Integration and Subordination

The Union was—or so it seemed to the Irish—a relationship of integration and subordination. This interpretation became immediately operative in Irish consciousness. Ireland became England-orientated. However, the Union, being in origin an expedient, did not produce any similar degree of impact on English consciousness. There was little if any appreciation that the formality of inclusion in the United Kingdom might have altered the status of Ireland as 'other'—subject, and essentially foreign. Thereafter, for England, the relationship had a conveniently dual complexion: Ireland could be treated as an integral part of England, or as distinct from it, whichever suited prevailing political or economic convenience. The differing Irish and English attitudes towards the Union are readily explicable in terms of the relative dimensions occupied by that arrangement in the affairs of the two countries. It was of paramount significance for Ireland, and of relatively minor importance in the affairs of imperial Britain.

So it was that the Irish regarded the relationship with a consistent seriousness amounting to obsession, while among the English it might provoke casual levity, callous amused contempt, or uncomprehending dismissal. *The Times* could remark in 1846, as famine bit deep into Ireland: 'Without attributing the splendid qualities of the British lion wholly to the agency of beef-steaks, we may pronounce that a people that has been reared on solid edibles will struggle long and hard against the degradation of a poorer subsistence. . . . For our own part, we regard the potato blight as a blessing. When the Celts once cease to be potatophagi, they must become carnivorous. With the taste of meats will grow the appetite for them; with the appetite the readiness to earn them.'

In the early 1880s [British prime minister Benjamin] Disraeli put aside Irish discontent with a wave of his hand: 'There! if you say "Bo!" loud enough to a goose—the goose will go away.' The spectacle of the election of the Sinn Feiner, Arthur Griffith, from inside gaol in 1918 moved Ian Hay to enunciate the general principle that 'The redeeming feature of Irish politics lies in the fact that the grimmest tragedy is never far removed from the wildest farce.'

Against such attitudes—whose illustration might be multiplied indefinitely—can be set those English reactions which exhibited genuine concern and benevolence, though here the range of illustration is more limited. A good example is the Marquess of Anglesey, Lord Lieutenant of Ireland in the late 1820s and early 1830s. Anglesey was eventually to resign in disgust with British policy. His sympathy with the Irish is evident in his contention that 'no one can expect a whole population to lie down and starve patiently', but the need to assert such a proposition implies its disregard by others. Anglesey's solution to the Irish question was prompt application of conciliatory paternalism: 'Pat will do what he ought, if justice is done to him, and if the consideration of his miseries is not long delayed.' However, the continuing problem was, that the structure of parliamentary politics frustrated any programme of conciliatory reforms by introducing delays and diminutions. To achieve anything it was necessary to placate the defenders of the *status quo* at the same time as bowing to the need for reform, which was the basis of the frequent association of coercion with conciliation. English ministers took the view that politics was the art of the possible and that the Irish must see and accept that. The possible was bounded by the rights of property, the need to maintain order, the need to take account of vested interests and established institutions, as well as the necessity of proceeding cautiously in complex matters.

The English Perception of the Union

There was also the powerful extra factor, peculiar to the Irish situation, of a firmly entrenched Anglo-Irish and Scots Protestant ascendancy, preoccupied with their own self-interests and the maintenance of the *status quo*, and numerically dominant in the British administration of Ireland. In the matter of vested interests, the landlords are most obvious, but up to 1869, the Church of England was possibly just as important, being powerful in the English as well as the Irish establishment, sacred in its claims, and intimately involved with virtually every Irish grievance.

This review of the forces arrayed in defence of the Irish *status quo*, might be taken to imply the suggestion that British governments wished to alter the *status quo* in Ireland, but were prevented from doing so. Quite the contrary. They wished the *status quo* to remain, but were obliged, by the pressure of Irish agitation and disorder, to attempt to adjust the existing structure to ensure its smoother operation. Certainly there were not lacking Englishmen to protest in the English parliament against the coercion of Ireland, but usually this was on the English ground that such coercion contravened the constitution by infringing the rights of the subject—and of course these few critics were always overwhelmed. In those in England who did seek long-term solutions, and genuine reforms rather than stop-gap expedients, paternalism, even self-righteousness, was too often apparent. Of most of them might be said what [James] Bryce remarked to [William] Gladstone: 'He had a tendency to persuade himself, quite unconsciously, that the course he desired to take was a course which the public interest required. His acuteness soon found reasons for that course; the warmth of his emotions enforced the reasons. It was a dangerous tendency, but it does not impeach his honesty of purpose.'

The various exigencies of English politics and politicians were one source of trouble. Another was the lack of cooperation between the Dublin administration and the Westminster government. It was occasionally possible—as in the case of the 1831 Arms Bill—for Irish legislation to be introduced into parliament without being seen by either the Dublin administration or, indeed, the British cabinet. The effects of this kind of malfunction can be seen in the 1831 case: the government immediately modified the Bill, but this was too late to avoid an outburst of enraged Irish protest, led by [Daniel] O'Connell. Then there was the fact that initiative in Irish policy lay with Home Secretaries or Chief Secretaries whose interests and abilities (or lack of them) as well as personal attitudes and beliefs, were vital to Irish affairs. Few Home Secretaries were really interested in Ireland. Some, like Lord Melbourne in the early 1830s, were bored by Ireland, angered by its endemic violence, and essentially unwilling to work out any Irish policy. As to the Chief Secretaries, the most powerful centres of British decision-making within Ireland, not many had ability, and in any case their frequent brevity of tenure disrupted continuity: there were nine Chief Secretaries between 1800 and 1812.

The English image of the responsibilities of the Union was, then, a very circumscribed and flickering one. While the Irish lived with the relationship all the time, for it dominated their domestic day-to-day affairs, for England it was an external matter, only occasionally pressing. 'So with all this,' wrote James

Callaghan, referring to all the other matters which confronted him as Home Secretary in the winter of 1967–8, 'I had no occasion to seek more work or to go out and look at the problems of Northern Ireland, unless they forced themselves upon me.' However natural, the fact that England attended to Ireland only when it was compelled to, only when there was something patently wrong, had a range of unfortunate effects. It constantly reinforced the image of Ireland as being incurably violent, for violence was taken to be the disease, not merely a symptom. It was violence which attracted the attention of English politicians, it was violence which prompted press reportage, pamphleteering, parliamentary speeches, and, more recently, television coverage. . . .

Enduring Images

But it was the extreme images developed in times of violence that tended to endure, and such periods of quiet as there were swiftly dropped out of English consciousness to produce an image of constant turbulence. Ireland's propagandists fostered this by concentrating, for their English audiences, not on the humdrum or the ordinary, but on the spectacular and the dramatic. This publicizing in Britain of Irish crises and discontent had two opposed effects. To some extent, promotion of an image of Irish turbulence was self-defeating. From the English viewpoint, Irish instability appeared most abnormal, hence both contemptible and in need of remedy: the very fact of the existence of this unhappy state of affairs justified tough intervention to restore stability, or at least prevent its further erosion. Against this, parading the condition of Ireland in its most extreme forms did awaken in England if not any widespread sense of guilt, a feeling of some responsibility to heed grievances. Irish advocates were always keen to use the comments of English critics of Irish policies: these existed in substantial quantity, and although such critiques were often made in the context of an opposition scoring points off a government, their party political origins did not reduce their utility. The Irish were particularly adept at using what the British regarded as their greatest virtues as debating points against Irish policy. The turning of the basic principles of liberty and democracy and fair play and humane treatment and the like against Britain was particularly discomforting to English Liberals (J.S. Mill and Gladstone furnish good examples). Such Liberals, pricked by their consciences, and finding endemic Irish violence distasteful, did eventually feel obliged to pay attention. That this tactic was not decisive is largely explained by the fact that so many Englishmen who cherished these large principles would not concede that they applied, at least fully, to the particular situation of Ireland.

But much more than propaganda, or the insistence on principles, it was Irish violence that captured English attention. Obviously, the English refusal to attend to Ireland's problems short of their violent expression fostered that very violence which the English most deplored, at the same time as creating a most adverse atmosphere for any solution. Cardinal [John] Newman remarked in 1881: 'I wish with all my heart that the cruel injustices which have been inflicted on the Irish people should be utterly removed—but I don't think they go the best way to bring this about.' But what was the best way? Newman did not say. In theory the best way was some peaceful way. In practice, the only way in which the Irish could attract serious attention to grievances crucial to them was by resort to the threat of violence or its actual use. Even then, progress was short term. Anglo-Irish relations were analogous to the story of the leaking roof: when storms made attention imperative, the climate was against anything more than temporary repairs; when the weather cleared, the problem could be forgotten.

**Great Britain and Ireland Unite:
January 1, 1801**

The Text of the Act of Union

by William Pitt

On July 2, 1800, the British parliament, under the leadership of Prime Minister William Pitt, produced the Act of Union of Great Britain and Ireland. The provisions of the document included the following: Ireland was to be joined to Great Britain into a single kingdom called the United Kingdom; the Irish parliament was to be abolished, but the Irish would have representation in the British parliament; the official church of Ireland was to be the Anglican Church; Catholics would not be permitted to hold public office; and the Irish civil service and court system were to be kept intact.

Although both sides opposed the act, both the British and Irish parliaments passed it. The Act of Union was signed by Britain's King George III (reigned 1760–1820) in August 1800. The union of Great Britain and Ireland was effective on January 1, 1801. The union remained in place until 1922, when the southern counties of Ireland left the United Kingdom and became a separate country.

W hereas in pursuance of H.M.'s ["His Majesty"—at this time, King George III] most gracious recommendation to the two Houses of Parliament in Great Britain and Ireland respectively, to consider of such measures as might best tend to strengthen and consolidate the connection between the two Kingdoms, the two Houses of the Parliament of Great Britain and the two Houses of the Parliament of Ireland have severally agreed and resolved that, in order to promote and secure the essential interests

---

William Pitt, "The Act of Union," July 2, 1800 (40 Geo. III c. 67).

of Great Britain and Ireland, and to consolidate the strength, power and resources of the British Empire, it will be advisable to concur in such measures as may best tend to unite the two Kingdoms of Great Britain and Ireland into one Kingdom, in such a manner, and on such terms and conditions, as may be established by the Acts of the respective Parliaments of Great Britain and Ireland.

And whereas, in furtherance of the said Resolution, both Houses of the said two Parliaments respectively have likewise agreed upon certain Articles for effectuating and establishing the said purposes, in the tenor following:

Article First. That it be the first Article of the Union of the Kingdoms of Great Britain and Ireland, that the said Kingdoms of Great Britain and Ireland shall, upon the 1st day of January which shall be in the year of our Lord 1801, and for ever after, be united into one Kingdom, by the name of The United Kingdom of Great Britain and Ireland; and that the royal style and titles appertaining to the Imperial Crown of the said United Kingdom and its dependencies; and also the ensigns, armorial flags and banners thereof shall be such as H.M., by his royal Proclamation under the Great Seal of the United Kingdom, shall be pleased to appoint.

Article Second. That it be the second Article of Union, that the succession to the Imperial Crown of the said United Kingdom, and of the dominions thereunto belonging, shall continue limited and settled . . . according to the existing laws, and to the terms of union between England and Scotland.

Article Third. That it be the third Article of Union that the said United Kingdom be represented in one and the same Parliament, to be styled The Parliament of the United Kingdom of Great Britain and Ireland.

Article Fourth. That it be the fourth Article of Union that four Lords Spiritual of Ireland by rotation of sessions, and 28 Lords Temporal of Ireland elected for life by the peers of Ireland, shall be the number to sit and vote on the part of Ireland in the House of Lords of the Parliament of the United Kingdom; and 100 commoners (two for each County of Ireland, two for the City of Dublin, two for the City of Cork, one for the University of Trinity College, and one for each of the 31 most considerable Cities, Towns and Boroughs) be the number to sit and vote on the part of Ireland in the House of Commons of the Parliament of the United Kingdom:

That such Act as shall be passed in the Parliament of Ireland previous to the Union, to regulate the mode by which the Lords

Spiritual and Temporal, and the Commons, to serve in the Parliament of the United Kingdom on the part of Ireland, shall be summoned and returned to the said Parliament, shall be considered as forming part of the Treaty of the Union, and shall be incorporated in the Acts of the respective Parliaments by which the said Union shall be ratified and established.

That any person holding any peerage in Ireland now subsisting, or hereafter to be created, shall not thereby be disqualified from being elected to serve, if he shall so think fit . . . for any county, city or borough of Great Britain, in the House of Commons of the United Kingdom, unless he shall have been previously elected as above, to sit in the House of Lords of the United Kingdom; but that so long as such peer of Ireland shall so continue to be a member of the House of Commons, he shall not be entitled to the privilege of peerage, nor be capable of being elected to serve as a peer on the part of Ireland, or of voting at any such election; and that he shall be liable to be sued, indicted, proceeded against, and tried as a commoner, for any offence with which he may be charged.

That all questions touching the election of members to sit on the part of Ireland in the House of Commons of the United Kingdom shall be heard and decided in the same manner as questions touching such elections in Great Britain now are, or at any time hereafter shall by law be heard and decided, subject nevertheless to such particular regulations in respect of Ireland as, from local circumstances, the Parliament of the United Kingdom may from time to time deem expedient.

That the qualifications in respect of property of the members elected on the part of Ireland to sit in the House of Commons of the United Kingdom, shall be respectively the same as are now provided by law in the cases of elections for counties and cities and boroughs respectively in that part of the United Kingdom called England, unless any other provision shall hereafter be made in that respect by Act of Parliament of the United Kingdom. . . .

That when H.M., his heirs or successors, shall declare his, her, or their pleasure for holding the first or any subsequent Parliament of the United Kingdom, a Proclamation shall issue, under the Great Seal of the United Kingdom, to cause the Lords Spiritual and Temporal, and Commons, who are to serve in the Parliament thereof on the part of Ireland, to be returned in such manner as by any Act of this present Session of the Parliament of Ireland shall be provided; and that the Lords Spiritual and Temporal and Commons of

Great Britain shall together with the Lords Spiritual and Temporal and Commons so returned as aforesaid on the part of Ireland, constitute the two Houses of the Parliament of the United Kingdom.

Article Fifth. That it be the fifth Article of Union, that the Churches of England and Ireland, as now by law established, be united into one Protestant Episcopal Church, to be called, The United Church of England and Ireland; and that the doctrine, worship, discipline and government of the said United Church shall be, and shall remain in full force for ever, as the same are now by law established for the Church of England; and that the continuance and preservation of the said united Church, as the Established Church of England and Ireland, shall be deemed and taken to be an essential and fundamental part of the Union; and that in like manner the doctrine, worship, discipline and government of the Church of Scotland shall remain and be preserved as the same are now established by law, and by the Acts for the Union of the two kingdoms of England and Scotland.

Article Sixth. That it be the sixth Article of Union, that H.M.'s subjects of Great Britain and Ireland shall, from and after the first day of January 1801 be entitled to the same privileges, and be on the same footing, as to encouragements and bounties on the like articles being the growth, produce or manufacture of either country respectively, and generally in respect of trade and navigation in all ports and places in the United Kingdom and its dependencies; and that in all treaties made by H.M., his heirs and successors with any foreign Power, H.M.'s subjects of Ireland shall have the same privileges and be on the same footing as H.M.'s subjects of Great Britain.

Article Seventh. That it be the seventh Article of Union, that the charge arising from the payment of interest, and the sinking fund for the reduction of the principal, of the debt incurred in either kingdom before the Union, shall continue to be separately defrayed by Great Britain and Ireland respectively, except as hereinafter provided: that for the space of 20 years after the Union shall take place, the contribution of Great Britain and Ireland respectively towards the expenditure of the United Kingdom in each year shall be defrayed in the proportion of fifteen parts for Great Britain, and two parts for Ireland; and that at the expiration of the said 20 years, the future expenditure of the United Kingdom (other than the interest and charges of the debt to which either country shall be separately liable) shall be defrayed in such proportion as the Parliament of the

United Kingdom shall deem just and reasonable upon a comparison of the real value of the exports and imports of the respective countries, upon an average of the three years next preceding the period of revision; or on a comparison of the value of the quantities of the following articles consumed within the respective countries, on a similar average; *videlicet* [that is], beer, spirits, sugar, wine, tea, tobacco and malt; or according to the aggregate proportion resulting from both these considerations combined; or on a comparison of the amount of income in each country, estimated from the produce for the same period of a general tax, if such shall have been imposed on the same descriptions of income in both countries; and that the Parliament of the United Kingdom shall afterwards proceed in like manner to revise and fix the said proportions according to the same rules, or any of them, at periods not more distant than 20 years, nor less than seven years from each other; unless, previous to any such period, the Parliament of the United Kingdom shall have declared, as hereinafter, provided, that the expenditure of the United Kingdom shall be defrayed indiscriminately, by equal taxes imposed on the like articles in both countries.

Article Eighth. That it be the eighth Article of Union, that all laws in force at the time of the Union, and all the courts of civil and ecclesiastical jurisdiction within the respective kingdoms, shall remain as now by law established within the same, subject only to such alterations and regulations from time to time as circumstances may appear to the Parliament of the United Kingdom to require.

And whereas the said Articles having, by Address of the respective Houses of Parliament in Great Britain and Ireland, been humbly laid before H.M., H.M. has been graciously pleased to approve the same; and to recommend it to his two Houses of Parliament in Great Britain and Ireland to consider of such measures as may be necessary for giving effect to the said Articles: in order, therefore, to give full effect and validity to the same, be it enacted . . . that the said foregoing recited Articles, each and every one of them, according to the true import and tenor thereof, be ratified, confirmed and approved, and be and they are hereby declared to be the Articles of the Union of Great Britain and Ireland, and the same shall be in force and have effect for ever, from the first day of Jan. . . . 1801; provided that before that period an Act shall have been passed by the Parliament of Ireland, for carrying into effect, in the like manner, the said foregoing recited Articles.

**Thomas Jefferson Assumes the Presidency:
1801**

A New Approach to Democracy

by Thomas Jefferson

Although few people then alive would have understood its significance, one event from the years 1800–1801 stands out as truly significant for the coming century.

In 1800 the United States counted for very little in world affairs. Its population of a little more than 4 million (almost a quarter of them black slaves) was spread out mainly in Atlantic seaboard states, and settlers were crossing the Appalachian Mountains to settle the Mississippi River lower basin only in places. Its economy was mainly localized; for most states, trade with Great Britain was more important than with neighboring states. There was little sense of national cohesion, and the new federal Constitution that had gone into force at the beginning of 1789 still seemed a tenuous experiment. Partisan and regional rancor ran high; defenders and haters of revolutionary France were at each other's throats, civil liberties were under attack as a result of the Alien and Sedition Laws of 1798, and there was talk of breaking up the Union. The 1800 presidential election was a bitter contest between the Federalist and Democratic Republican Parties, which disagreed fundamentally over whether democracy was a good thing. Because of a flawed provision in the Constitution (which had not envisioned the existence of competitive political parties), the two top contenders for the presidency were deadlocked in the electoral college as the year 1800 closed. Whether a president could even be inaugurated in March 1801, as scheduled, seemed questionable. The raw new American republic, isolated three thousand miles across the Atlantic on the outer fringe of the Western world, might well not survive. And if it failed, few in Europe would have mourned.

Thomas Jefferson, first inaugural address, 1801.

But survive it did. Thanks to the good sense of a few moderate Federalists, one vote shifted in Congress, which sufficed to permit Thomas Jefferson (1743–1826) to be formally elected president and to take the oath of office. Partisan rancor by no means disappeared, but because Jefferson and his victorious Republicans believed that government should be as weak and decentralized as possible, there were no serious reprisals against the losing Federalists—who indeed began to fade away as an organized party. Probably the United States owed its continued existence in those early years to the "antipower" beliefs of the dominant Republican Party. Whatever the reason, history's first peaceful transfer of political power between bitter political rivals had occurred as a result of the election of 1800, and the United States had a new lease on life. In the century to come, it would grow into a full-fledged democracy, an industrial giant, a continental nation stretching from the Atlantic to the Pacific and beyond. By 1900 it would stand poised to become the greatest power on the globe.

Jefferson's first inaugural address envisaged few of the dramatic changes that would transform the United States in the century to come. But as a testimonial to the hope of purposely keeping government as limited as possible, Jefferson gave voice to the ideals that would in fact permit the United States to make the transition to democracy and thus to what his great successor Abraham Lincoln would call "the last, best hope of earth."

During the contest of opinion through which we have passed the animation of discussions and of exertions has sometimes worn an aspect which might impose on strangers unused to think freely and to speak and to write what they think; but this being now decided by the voice of the nation, announced according to the rules of the Constitution, all will, of course, arrange themselves under the will of the law, and unite in common efforts for the common good. All, too, will bear in mind this sacred principle, that though the will of the majority is in all cases to prevail, that will to be rightful must be reasonable; that the minority possess their equal rights, which equal law must protect, and to violate would be oppression. Let us, then, fellow-citizens, unite with one heart and one mind. Let us restore to social intercourse that harmony and affection without which liberty and even life itself are but dreary things. And let us reflect that, having banished from our land that religious intolerance under which mankind so long bled and suffered, we have yet gained little if we countenance a political intolerance as despotic, as wicked, and capable of as bitter and bloody persecutions. During the throes and convulsions of the ancient world, during the agonizing spasms of infuriated man, seeking through blood and slaughter his long-lost liberty, it was not wonderful that the agitation of the billows should reach even this distant and peaceful shore; that this should be more felt and feared by some and less by others, and should divide opinions as to measures of safety. But every difference of opinion is not a difference of principle. We have called by different names brethren of the same principle. We are all Republicans, we are all Federalists. If there be any among us who would wish to dissolve this Union or to change its republican form, let them stand undisturbed as monuments of the safety with which error of opinion may be tolerated where reason is left free to combat it. I know, indeed, that some honest men fear that a republican government can not be strong, that this Government is not strong enough; but would the honest patriot, in the full tide of successful experiment, abandon a government which has so far kept us free and firm on the theoretic and visionary fear that this Government, the world's best hope, may by possibility want energy to preserve itself? I trust not. I believe this, on the contrary, the strongest Government on earth. I believe it the only one where every man, at the call of the law, would fly to the standard of the law, and would meet invasions of the public order as his own personal concern. Sometimes it is said that man can not be trusted with the government of himself. Can he, then, be trusted with the government of others? Or have we found angels in the forms of kings to govern him? Let history answer this question.

Let us, then, with courage and confidence pursue our own Federal and Republican principles, our attachment to union and representative government. Kindly separated by nature and a wide ocean from the exterminating havoc of one quarter of the globe; too high-minded to endure the degradations of the others; possessing a chosen country, with room enough for our descendants to the thousandth and thousandth generation; entertaining a due sense of our equal right to the use of our own faculties, to the acquisitions of our own industry, to honor and confidence from our fellow-citizens, resulting not from birth, but from our actions and their sense of them; enlightened by a benign religion, professed, indeed, and practiced in various forms, yet all of them inculcating honesty, truth, temperance, gratitude, and the love of man; acknowledging and adoring an overruling Providence, which by all its dispensations proves that it delights in the happiness of man here and his greater happiness hereafter—with all these blessings, what more is necessary to make us a happy and a prosperous people? Still one thing more, fellow-citizens—a wise and frugal Government, which shall restrain men from injuring one another, shall leave them otherwise free to regulate their own pursuits of industry and improvement, and shall not take from the mouth of labor the bread it has earned. This is the sum of good government, and this is necessary to close the circle of our felicities.

About to enter, fellow-citizens, on the exercise of duties which comprehend everything dear and valuable to you, it is proper you should understand what I deem the essential principles of our Government, and consequently those which ought to shape its Administration. I will compress them within the narrowest compass they will bear, stating the general principle, but not all its limitations. Equal and exact justice to all men, of whatever state or persuasion, religious or political; peace, commerce, and honest friendship with all nations, entangling alliances with none; the support of the State governments in all their rights, as the most competent administrations for our domestic concerns and the surest bulwarks against anti-republican tendencies; the preservation of the General Government in its whole constitutional vigor, as the sheet anchor of our peace at home and safety abroad; a jealous care of the right of election by the people—a mild and safe corrective of abuses which are lopped by the sword of revolution where peaceable remedies are unprovided; absolute acquiescence in the decisions of the majority, the vital principle of republics, from which is no appeal but to force, the vital principle and immediate parent of despotism; a well-disciplined militia, our best reliance in peace and for the first moments of war, till regulars may relieve them; the supremacy of the civil over the military authority; economy in the public expense, that labor may be lightly burthened; the honest payment of our debts and sacred preservation of the public faith; encouragement of agriculture, and of commerce as its handmaid; the diffusion of information and arraignment of all abuses at the bar of the public reason; freedom of religion; freedom of the press, and freedom of person under the protection of the habeas corpus, and trial by juries impartially selected. These principles form the bright constellation which has gone before us and guided our steps through an age of revolution and reformation. The wisdom of our sages and blood of our heroes have been devoted to their attainment. They should be the creed of our political faith, the text of civic instruction, the touchstone by which to try the services of those we trust; and should we wander from them in moments of error or of alarm, let us hasten to retrace our steps and to regain the road which alone leads to peace, liberty, and safety.

The United States and France Negotiate the
Louisiana Purchase: April 30, 1803

The Louisiana Purchase Changed the United States Geographically and Culturally

by Jon Kukla

On April 30, 1803, France negotiated the sale of Louisiana to the
United States. Napoléon Bonaparte was interested in selling
Louisiana to the United States for several reasons. His failed conquest of the West Indian island Santo Domingo rendered Louisiana
useless as a supply base for the region. Napoléon also wished to re-
sume war with Great Britain, and the sale of Louisiana would provide money for war.

Negotiations between Robert Livingston and James Monroe of
the United States and the Marquis Francis Barbé Marbois of France
resulted in a treaty dated April 30, 1803. The Louisiana Purchase
not only nearly doubled the size of the United States, but also, it set
a precedent for the acquisition of foreign land and peoples through
a negotiated treaty.

The following selection by Jon Kukla reflects on the Louisiana
Purchase and its reception by the American public. Kukla also dis-

Jon Kukla, *So Immense: The Louisiana Purchase and the Destiny of America*. New York:
Alfred A. Knopf, 2003. Copyright © 2003 by Jon Kukla. All rights reserved. Reproduced by
permission of Alfred A. Knopf, Inc., a division of Random House, Inc.

cusses the ways in which the purchase changed the United States, both geographically and socially.

Historian Jon Kukla, author of several books, is the director of the Patrick Henry Memorial Foundation in Virginia.

A t dawn on Saturday, May 11,1804, cannon sounded a "Grand National Salute" from the Battery at the tip of Manhattan and the fort on nearby Governors Island as New York City launched a grand celebration of the first anniversary of the Louisiana Purchase Treaty. The event was orchestrated by the city's new mayor, and former United States senator, De Witt Clinton. American flags were visible everywhere, flying over the principal buildings of the city and from the masts of all the ships in the harbor. As church bells pealed in triumph, Mayor Clinton, the sheriff, and scores of municipal officials gathered in City Hall Park for a gigantic parade. Rank upon rank of militiamen—cavalry, infantry, and artillery—marched through the streets of Manhattan behind their commander, who rode a profusely decorated white stallion as he held up the front end of a very long white silk banner inscribed with the words: "Extension of the Empire of Freedom in the Peaceful, Honorable, and Glorious Acquisition of the Immense and Fertile Region of Louisiana, December 20th, 1803, 28th Year of American Independence, and in the Presidency of Thomas Jefferson."

Celebrating the Louisiana Purchase

Behind the soldiers and politicians came the members of New York's Tammany Society, carrying a fifteen-foot-long white muslin map of the Mississippi River and the territory of Louisiana. As the procession marched through lower Manhattan, cannons roared salutes to the three nations, and bands played rousing music, including "Hail, Columbia," an unnamed "Spanish piece," and "Bonaparte's March." At last the parade turned back up Broadway and arrived again at City Hall Park, where the soldiers fired crisp salutes and the assembled populace gave three resounding cheers for Thomas Jefferson and the Louisiana Purchase.

Seven hundred miles to the south on the next day, May 12, the southern Federalist Dr. David Ramsay, the most able historian of the nation's founding generation, was mounting the pulpit of St. Michael's Church in Charleston, South Carolina, to deliver his *Oration on the Cession of Louisiana to the United States.* Ramsay was one of dozens of orators in cities and towns up and down the Eastern Seaboard raising their voices in a jubilee of oratory in the spring of 1804 to celebrate the one-year anniversary of the Louisiana Purchase.

"Louisiana is Ours!" David Ramsay proclaimed. As to the significance of America's acquisition of that vast territory, Ramsay acknowledged "the establishment of independence, and of our present constitution" as "prior, both in time and importance; but with these two exceptions," Ramsay believed, "the acquisition of Louisiana, is the greatest political blessing ever conferred on these states."

Historical perspective had not changed much one hundred forty-nine years later when the Pulitzer Prize–winning historian and "Easy Chair" columnist for *Harper's* magazine, Bernard DeVoto, wrote an essay commissioned by *Collier's* magazine about the Louisiana Purchase upon the occasion of its sesquicentennial in 1953. Because he lived after the shots at Fort Sumter and surrender at Appomattox, DeVoto added one event to the comparative list, but otherwise his opinion about the Louisiana Purchase echoed Ramsay's:

> No event in all American history—not the Civil War, nor the Declaration of Independence nor even the signing of the Constitution—was more important.

DeVoto wrote about westward expansion, exploration, and commerce, and he wrote about constitutional change and the Civil War, and he came close to proving his point. But Bernard DeVoto knew that something was missing. "However it may be put," he lamented, the peaceful transfer of sovereignty from Spain, to France, to the United States for nine hundred thousand square miles of territory was a story "still too momentous to be understood."

A Noble Bargain

Despite some misgivings about the constitutional issues, most Americans agreed that the Louisiana Purchase was, in [nineteenth-century French statesman Charles Maurice de] Talleyrand's words, "a noble bargain"—*la bonne affaire!* The Mississippi and its western tributaries alone drain a million square miles. The price of securing the Ohio-Mississippi waterway and doubling the size of the United States was 80 million francs ($15 million) financed for twenty years by the Barings Bank of London and Hope & Co. of Amsterdam. International negotiations, completed in 1819, refined the boundaries between American and Spanish territories and also transferred Florida to the United States.

Still, $15 million was a lot of money at the beginning of the nineteenth century, especially to strict-constructionist Jeffersonians paying off the national debt that Alexander Hamilton had created to strengthen the central government. "Some people have expressed fears lest our government may have given too much for Louisiana," a New Jersey wit advised the editors of the Trenton *True American:*

> I would wish you to inform your readers that a company of monied men in this and the neighboring states is forming, for the purpose of purchasing Louisiana [from] our government . . . for the purchase money and the expence of the negotiation.

They would have made a killing. When the 6 percent loans were repaid, the total cost of Mississippi navigation and the whole Louisiana Territory was $23,527,872.57—about 4 cents an acre.

Millions of acres of cheap fresh lands drained by the Mississippi and its tributaries were ideal for cotton—a commodity with a lucrative new market in the steam-driven mills of Manchester, a fiber readily processed by Eli Whitney's cotton gin, and a crop well suited to plantation agriculture and slave labor. . . .

Louisiana and Controversies

When [first governor of Louisiana] William C.C. Claiborne's ancestors had landed at Jamestown in 1616, English colonists regarded the lands they took in North America (as earlier in Ulster) as a wilderness peopled only with savages, the remnants of Native American tribes decimated by European disease. Thomas Jefferson lived in a plantation community of two hundred people on his mountaintop at Monticello. He walked daily among faces that exhibited a whole range of tones, even within his own family, but Jefferson saw only white and black, free and slave. The "amalgamation" of black Americans "with the other color," he wrote in 1814, "produces a degradation to which no lover of his country, no lover of excellence in the human character can innocently consent." His representatives and his countrymen brought similar attitudes to their 1803 encounter with the racial diversity of Louisiana.

Claiborne and the twelve thousand Americans who flooded into Louisiana in the decade after 1803 almost overwhelmed New Orleans's baffling patterns of race, language, law, and culture. Jef-

ferson and his countrymen had always assumed that the Creoles would be displaced, assimilated, or marginalized by English-speaking settlers—and they might have been, except for the aftermath of the Haitian and French Revolutions. Between May 1809 and January 1810, New Orleans welcomed ten thousand French-speaking refugees from St. Domingue by way of Cuba—equal numbers of whites, slaves, and free people of color whose arrival made the city even more Caribbean, reinforcing everything that Claiborne and his countrymen found exotic and dangerous about New Orleans for decades to come.

Controversies over race, religion, law, language, and culture not only delayed Louisiana's statehood until 1812, they worked like the rumblings of an earthquake along the vulnerable fault lines of nineteenth-century American society and government. By 1818–1819, when treaties among the United States, Spain, and Great Britain gave America the rest of Florida and drew the final boundaries of the Louisiana Purchase, the second half of our national history was well under way. The land north of the thirty-third parallel was now called the Missouri Territory, to avoid confusion with the State of Louisiana south of it.

As Americans brought their internal improvements and their slaves to New Orleans and the new territory, the nation's long-deferred debate over slavery grew increasingly angry. The consequences of the Louisiana Purchase scoured at the mortar of the Constitution, as the New Englanders' arguments for state rights and secession—arguments that surfaced during the Jay-Gardoqui negotiations [between the United States and Spain] of 1786, after the Louisiana Purchase in 1803–1804, and again during the War of 1812—went south.

In 1820, when the Missouri crisis erupted over the creation of another slave state from the territory of the Louisiana Purchase, a grand compromise was necessary to preserve the union: henceforth the new states were admitted in pairs, one slave and one free, to keep a balance of power in the Senate. This Missouri Compromise worked until the 1850s, but the Missouri Question (as the "Louisiana Question" had come to be known, to avoid confusion) haunted the conscience of America until the cannon roared at Fort Sumter—and long beyond.

Implications of the Louisiana Purchase

Americans today live their lives in the wake of the Louisiana Purchase. It reshaped our hemisphere so completely that we cannot easily imagine anything different. It spurred exploration and expansion. It lured the republic toward the temptations of empire. Lewis and Clark tracked the northern reaches of the vast territory in 1804–1806 and staked a claim to the Pacific Northwest. [Soldier and explorer] Zebulon Pike and others headed south and west. The landscape inspired artists from George Caleb Bingham and George Catlin to Thomas Hart Benton, Ansel Adams, and Georgia O'Keeffe. A nation that once may have been resigned to sharing the Mississippi with a foreign neighbor now embraced the Pacific Coast as its "Manifest Destiny." But DeVoto knew all this in 1953 when he said the event was "still too momentous to be understood." He knew the Louisiana Purchase brought geographic expansion, discovery and exploration, and sectional and constitutional conflicts that led to the Civil War. And he sensed that something was missing.

As we mark the two hundredth anniversary of the Louisiana Purchase, our vantage point suggests that David Ramsay and Bernard DeVoto were too close to their subject—too close in time—to comprehend its momentous implications. Even as recently as 1953, one hundred fifty years after the event, some of the long-term consequences of the Louisiana Purchase were not yet apparent. Today, as its two hundredth anniversary converges upon the four hundredth anniversaries of Jamestown Island and Plymouth Rock, our perspective may be clearer simply because we and our children have lived longer with the results of the Louisiana Purchase.

How different the United States was for our parents and grandparents in 1953: Eight of ten Americans then lived on a farm or in a small town; today eight of ten live in urban areas. The Korean War was ending. French soldiers were losing a war in Vietnam. Joseph Stalin was in the final year of his life, and Joseph McCarthy in the final year of his credibility. Fidel Castro was an obscure prisoner in a Cuban jail. Neither the Berlin Wall nor the Watergate Hotel had been built. Color television was experimental, and only 29 percent of American women worked outside the home, compared with 57 percent today. Spanish was a foreign language. Segregation was the law in the American south and widely practiced throughout the country. *Brown v. Topeka* [the 1954 Supreme Court case that led to the desegregation of schools] was in the lower courts. The Salk vaccine [for polio] was in field tests, and the Pill was just a dream. Today, in short, we have a vantage point denied to David Ramsay in 1804 and Bernard DeVoto in 1953.

In the two centuries of Anglo-American colonial history from Jamestown to the Louisiana Purchase, American public life had become the domain of Protestant, agrarian, English-speaking men. Whites were free, blacks were slaves, and Native Americans did not count. Starting at New Orleans in 1803, five million Americans along the Atlantic Seaboard accelerated an encounter with diversity that has been sustained by geographic expansion and immigration in the nineteenth and twentieth centuries. Ramsay and DeVoto could not yet see it, but the Louisiana Purchase was a turning point at America's halfway mark toward an inclusive national history. Looking back from the year 2003, Americans should marvel at who we have become—the very antithesis of John Winthrop's Boston, Timothy Pickering's Salem, James Monroe's Virginia, or Thomas Jefferson's yeoman republic. We may wonder what the next two centuries have in store.

Encounter with Diversity

Travelers who actually visited New Orleans two centuries ago probably came closest to seeing the human significance of the Louisiana Purchase that eluded David Ramsay and Bernard DeVoto. The Jeffersonian polymath Benjamin Henry Latrobe, for example, arriving in 1819 to complete the construction of waterworks for the city of New Orleans, encountered "a more incessant, loud, rapid, and various gabble of tongues . . . than was ever heard at Babel." He found the three-caste society of New Orleans "wholly new even to one who has traveled much in Europe and America"—a bustling urban place filled with Catholics, Creoles, French, Spanish, Africans, Native Americans, West Indians, and Anglo-Americans. With Irish, Germans, and countless others soon to arrive. At the Cabildo in New Orleans on December 20, 1803, the United States began a long encounter with diversity that has forced us, and that should inspire us, to think and to live far differently than the Founders expected.

Although Ramsay and DeVoto did not have the imagination to envisage it, we live at a moment when census officials report that Spanish-speaking Americans have become the nation's largest minority group. Is it not time for Americans to look beyond the colonial East Coast dichotomy of black and white? Without forgetting that the Louisiana territory witnessed ugly and vicious moments of racial discord and bloodshed, we want to hope that perhaps—standing at the beginning of a millennium and on the eve of a bicentennial—perhaps we can learn a lesson from the good people of that *"Gallo-Hispano-Indian omnium gatherum* of savages and adventurers" who lived in the "unmeasured world beyond that river" and scared the dickens out of Fisher Ames [a founding father who advocated a constitutional republic].

If a candid reconsideration of the Louisiana Purchase helps us see diversity rather than dichotomy in the history we share with one another and with the world, perhaps we Americans can begin to look back at the Louisiana Purchase as a tributary in a long and slow and often tragic story of eventual inclusion. And perhaps the most fascinating part of the story of the Louisiana Purchase—the destiny of America—remains farther downstream.

The Text of the Agreement Between France and the United States

by Robert R. Livingston, James Monroe, and Francis Barbé Marbois

Talks between the Marquis Francis Barbé Marbois (Napoléon's minister of finance) and Robert R. Livingston (U.S. minister to Paris) and James Monroe (envoy extraordinary and minister plenipotentiary to France) lasted from April 11 to May 9, 1803. The official agreement negotiating the sale of French Louisiana to the United States, dated April 30, 1803, consisted of a treaty and two conventions. In addition to the acquisition of Louisiana by the United States, the treaty terms stated that the United States was to pay France approximately $15 million, the inhabitants of the territory were to be incorporated into the United States, and these inhabitants were to be accorded all the rights of U.S. citizens. The effective transfer of lower Louisiana to the United States took place on December 20, 1803; upper Louisiana was officially transferred on March 10, 1804.

The Louisiana Purchase, which included 828,000 square miles, nearly doubled the size of the United States. Eventually, all or part of thirteen states were carved from this territory, which stretched

---

Robert R. Livingston, James Monroe, and Francis Barbé Marbois, treaty between the United States of America and the French Republic, April 30, 1803.

from the Mississippi River westward to the Rocky Mountains. Canada formed the northern border of the territory while the Gulf of Mexico formed the southern one. Over time, seven places in the Louisiana territory were given the name Jefferson in honor of the U.S. president who effected the purchase.

The President of the United States of America and the First Consul of the French Republic in the name of the French People desiring to remove all Source of misunderstanding relative to objects of discussion mentioned in the second and fifth articles of the Convention of the 8th Vendémiaire an 9/30 September 1800 relative to the rights claimed by the United States in virtue of the Treaty concluded at Madrid the 27 of October 1795, between His Catholic Majesty and the Said United States, and willing to Strengthen the union and friendship which at the time of the Said Convention was happily reestablished between the two nations have respectively named their Plenipotentiaries to wit. The President of the United States, by and with the advice and consent of the Senate of the Said States; Robert R. Livingston Minister Plenipotentiary of the United States and James Monroe Minister Plenipotentiary and Envoy extraordinary of the Said States near the Government of the French Republic; And the First Consul in the name of the French people, Citizen Francis Barbé Marbois Minister of the public treasury who after having respectively exchanged their full powers have agreed to the following Articles.

Article I

Whereas by the Article the third of the Treaty concluded at St Ildefonso the 9th Vendémiaire an 9/1st October 1800 between the First Consul of the French Republic and his Catholic Majesty it was agreed as follows.

"His Catholic Majesty promises and engages on his part to cede to the French Republic six months after the full and entire execution of the conditions and Stipulations herein relative to his Royal Highness the Duke of Parma, the Colony or Province of Louisiana with the Same extent that it now has in the hand of Spain, and that it had when France possessed it; and Such as it Should be after the Treaties subsequently entered into between Spain and other States."

And whereas in pursuance of the Treaty and particularly of the third article the French Republic has an incontestable title to the domain and to the possession of the said Territory—The First Consul of the French Republic desiring to give to the United States a strong proof of his friendship doth hereby cede to the United States in the name of the French Republic for ever and in full Sovereignty the said territory with all its rights and appurtenances as fully and in the Same manner as they have been acquired by the French Republic in virtue of the above mentioned Treaty concluded with his Catholic Majesty.

Article II

In the cession made by the preceding article are included the adjacent Islands belonging to Louisiana all public lots and Squares, vacant lands and all public buildings, fortifications, barracks and other edifices which are not private property.—The Archives, papers and documents relative to the domain and Sovereignty of Louisiana and its dependences will be left in the possession of the Commissaries of the United States, and copies will be afterwards given in due form to the Magistrates and Municipal officers of Such of the said papers and documents as may be necessary to them.

Article III

The inhabitants of the ceded territory shall be incorporated in the Union of the United States and admitted as soon as possible according to the principles of the federal Constitution to the enjoyment of all the rights, advantages and immunities of citizens of the United States, and in the mean time they shall be maintained and protected in the free enjoyment of their liberty, property and the Religion which they profess.

Article IV

There Shall be Sent by the Government of France a Commissary to Louisiana to the end that he do every act necessary as well to receive from the Officers of his Catholic Majesty the Said country and its dependences in the name of the French Republic if it has not been already done as to transmit it in the name of the French Republic to the Commissary or agent of the United States.

Article V

Immediately after the ratification of the present Treaty by the President of the United States and in case that of the first Consul's shall have been previously obtained, the Commissary of the French Republic shall remit all military posts of New Orleans and other parts of the ceded territory to the Commissary or Commissaries named by the President to take possession—the troops whether of France or Spain who may be there shall cease to occupy any military post from the time of taking possession and shall be embarked as soon as possible in the course of three months after the ratification of this treaty.

Article VI

The United States promise to execute Such treaties and articles as may have been agreed between Spain and the tribes and nations of Indians until by mutual consent of the United States and the said tribes or nations other Suitable articles Shall have been agreed upon.

Article VII

As it is reciprocally advantageous to the commerce of France and the United States to encourage the communication of both nations for a limited time in the country ceded by the present treaty until general arrangements relative to the commerce of both nations may be agreed on; it has been agreed between the contracting parties that the French Ships coming directly from France or any of her colonies loaded only with the produce and manufactures of France or her Said Colonies; and the Ships of Spain coming directly from Spain or any of her colonies loaded only with the produce or manufactures of Spain or her Colonies shall be admitted during the Space of twelve years in in [sic] the Port of New Orleans and in all other legal ports-of-entry within the ceded territory in the Same manner as the Ships of the United States coming directly from France or Spain or any of their Colonies without being Subject to any other or greater duty on merchandize or other or greater tonnage than that paid by the citizens of the United States.

During the Space of time above mentioned no other nation Shall have a right to the Same privileges in the Ports of the ceded territory—the twelve years Shall commence three months after the exchange of ratifications if it Shall take place in France or three months after it Shall have been notified at Paris to the French Government if it Shall take place in the United States; It is however well understood that the object of the above article is to favour the manufactures, Commerce, freight and navigation of France and of Spain So far as relates to the importations that the

French and Spanish Shall make into the Said Ports of the United States without in any Sort affecting the regulations that the United States may make concerning the exportation of the produce and merchandize of the United States, or any right they may have to make Such regulations.

Article VIII

In future and for ever after the expiration of the twelve years, the Ships of France shall be treated upon the footing of the most favoured nations in the ports above mentioned.

Article IX

The particular Convention Signed this day by the respective Ministers having for its object to provide for the payment of debts due to the Citizens of the United States by the French Republic prior to the 30th September 1800 (8th Vendémiaire an 9) is approved and to have its execution in the Same manner as if it had been inserted in this present treaty, and it Shall be ratified in the same form and in the Same time So that the one Shall not be ratified distinct from the other.

Another particular Convention Signed at the Same date as the present treaty relative to a definitive rule between the contracting parties is in the like manner approved and will be ratified in the Same form, and in the Same time and jointly.

Article X

The present treaty Shall be ratified in good and due form and the ratifications Shall be exchanged in the Space of Six months after the date of the Signature by the Ministers Plenipotentiary or Sooner if possible.

In faith whereof the respective Plenipotentiaries have Signed these articles in the French and English languages; declaring nevertheless that the present Treaty was originally agreed to in the French language; and have thereunto affixed their Seals.

Done at Paris the tenth day of Floreal in the eleventh year of the French Republic; and the 30th of April 1803.

Robt R Livingston [seal]
Jas Monroe [seal]
Barbé Marbois [seal]

The World and France React to the Emperor

by Leo Gershoy

The years following the French Revolution of 1789, which toppled the monarchy in France, were characterized by political and social instability. By the late 1790s, Napoléon Bonaparte, who had risen through the military ranks to become a general, took on a leadership role in tumultuous France. Between 1800 and 1804 he ruled as dictator and was a popular figure with the public. In May 1804, the French people voted in favor of the creation of an empire to be led by Napoléon.

The coronation was held on December 2, 1804. Napoléon, who was supposed to be crowned emperor by Pope Pius VII, surprised everyone by placing the crown on his own head. He also crowned the new empress, his wife Josephine. During his reign as emperor (1804–1814), Napoléon centralized the government, created a modern bureaucracy, nationalized the police system, stabilized the financial system, and promoted industry. Two Napoleonic reforms with a long-lasting legacy were the codification of the law and the centralized education system.

Through military means, Napoléon also established the largest empire since that of ancient Rome. His army was composed of two hundred thousand men, both professional officers and volunteers. The emperor also employed innovative military strategies by never using the same methods twice; rather, he derived new tactics by

Leo Gershoy, *The French Revolution and Napoleon*. New York: Appleton-Century-Crofts, Inc., 1933. Copyright © 1933 by F.S. Crofts & Co., Inc. Renewed in 1970 by Dr. Leo Gershoy. Reproduced by permission of Simon & Schuster, Inc.

evaluating each situation independently.

The following excerpt by Leo Gershoy illuminates the process by which the imperial title was created. Gershoy puts into this context the significance of a plot against Napoléon's life. The author describes both the politics of the newly minted French empire as well as the European monarchs' reactions to Napoléon's ascendancy.

Professor Leo Gershoy was a specialist in European history who was affiliated with New York University for over thirty-five years.

The life consulate [a top-level governmental position] was only a stop-gap of two years' duration, an interval which Bonaparte employed to good advantage in furthering his personal interests. The success of his sweeping reforms in internal affairs swelled the popularity that he gained by restoration of order in France and his termination of the war. With the exception of the few uncompromising Jacobins, who were quiet, and the royalists, who were soon to be discredited, all classes sang his praise. He seemed a bulwark against disorder. Yet his life was still endangered by secret conspiracies, although, since the explosion of the "infernal machine" [an assassination attempt against him] in 1800, he had taken the most careful precautions and never showed himself in public without a large escort of police. The most famous of the plots against him, which was disclosed in 1804, bears examination, for it was the suppression of the conspiracy which gave Bonaparte the opportunity to make his rule hereditary.

A Manufactured Plot

Toward the end of 1803, various royalist emigrants living in London drew up an elaborate plan involving uprisings in the west and south of France, the abduction or assassination of the first consul, and the return of a Bourbon pretender to France. From supposedly royalist sources in France the émigré conspirators received funds, and from the mouth of a presumed French royalist they obtained firm assurances that the republican opposition in France would join them against Bonaparte. As we now know, Bonaparte himself supplied the funds, while the French royalist who gave them assurances was a secret agent of [Joseph] Fouché, Bonaparte's former minister. In short, the first consul manufactured a plot which at all times he controlled and which he could disclose when disclosure served his ends.

The occasion came early in 1804, when the Breton, Georges Cadoudal, and General [Jean] Pichegru, the leaders of the conspiracy, secretly met General [Jean] Moreau in Paris and tried to win his support. All three were arrested and imprisoned, Moreau unjustly, for he had refused to join the conspirators. While the press bared the horrible details of what seemed a dastardly plot, the government's secret police hunted high and low for the Bourbon prince who was expected in France. They knew that it could not be the count of Artois, who had not budged from England, so they sought to pick up the scent elsewhere. The trail led to Baden, where the young prince of Enghien, the grandson of the duke of Condé, was living. It was reported that he came secretly into Strasbourg, received secret English agents, and was in communication with the traitor [Charles] Dumouriez. Upon the receipt of these reports, even before the arrest of Cadoudal, Bonaparte jumped to the conclusion that Dumouriez and Enghien were the active leaders (or dupes) of the plot. Inspired by [Charles] Talleyrand and Fouché, who were anxious to compromise him by a crime which would make him their accomplice and end his reproaches against their revolutionary past, Bonaparte made a grievous decision. He ordered his soldiers to invade the territory of Baden, seize Enghien, and speed him to Paris for trial. When he gave those orders he had already decided to condemn the young Bourbon to death. The arrest took place in the night of March 14. On the 20th, the last of the Condes was brought to the castle of Vincennes and a scant six hours after his arrvial, at eleven o'clock at night, he was subjected to the indignity of a hollow military trial. Before the break of dawn he was shot, and his body thrown into an open grave that had been dug before his arrival at Vincennes.

In the meantime, long before Enghien had reached Paris, the first consul had learned that the prince was entirely innocent. Why then did Bonaparte persevere in that act of extraordinary violence and crime which sullied his entire career? He never dodged the responsibility for this act. In his will he wrote:

> I caused the duke of Enghien to be arrested and judged, because it was necessary for the safety, the interest, and the honor of the French people when the count of Artois, by his own confession was supporting sixty assassins at Paris. Under similar circumstances I would again act in the same way.

In other words, the murder of the duke was at once an act of reprisal and a warning to the Bourbons, a terrible declaration that reconciliation between them and Bonaparte was impossible.

The punishment of the royalist conspirators soon followed. A fortnight after the execution of Enghien the hapless Pichegru was found strangled in his cell. Cadoudal and several other conspirators were condemned to death and executed. Moreau, whose quiet self-possession and dignity during the trial won the sympathy of the court and audience, was first condemned to a brief imprisonment and later pardoned on condition that he accept exile to America. Thus the first consul removed one of his dangerous military rivals and the leader of the moderate republican opposition.

Completing the Dictatorship

The horror that filled Paris at the news of the execution of the duke of Enghien found its echo in a temporary depression of the stock market and in a momentary decline of Bonaparte's great popularity. On the whole, the stirring events of the conspiracy, the trial, and the punishments rebounded in favor of that ambitious project which he had unceasingly nursed, the establishment of his hereditary rule. A current of opinion, in part genuine and in part sedulously inspired by the government, swept the country in favor of Bonaparte. His political henchmen guardedly advanced a project for the consolidation of his régime. They stressed the main argument that he and he alone stood between France and the renewal of the revolutionary upheaval. The peasantry, the military and the middle class for whom Bonaparte's rule meant prosperity and peace were quite indifferent to the secret intrigues which prepared the way for the establishment of the hereditary empire. Even those who had distaste for his methods and ambition felt that the moment had come for France to put an end to foreign intrigue and to make such changes as would place the stability of their government beyond the question of Bonaparte's continued existence or his sudden death at the hands of an assassin. The contemplated change was inevitable. It completed the dictatorship begun in Brumaire.

Within a week after the execution of Enghien, the Senate petitioned Bonaparte "to complete his work by rendering it, like his glory, immortal." While the first consul bided his time, allowing public opinion to seize the full implications of the Senate's petition, one of his admirers presented a motion in the Tribunate to have Napoleon Bonaparte proclaimed emperor and the imperial dignity declared hereditary in his family. Only [Lazare] Carnot, "the Organizer of Victory" of 1793, dared risk Bonaparte's wrath and speak against it. The Corps législatif meekly voted in favor of the project. On May 4 the Senate, to which the vote of the assembly had been communicated, declared: "Glory, gratitude, devotion reason, the interests of the state, all unite to proclaim Napoleon hereditary emperor." Napoleon then busied himself, as the head of the government committee, with drawing up a new constitutional document. After a short debate in the Council of State the document was transmitted to the Senate which adopted it as the "Organic Senatus Consultum of 28 Floréal, Year XII" (May 18, 1804).

During his reign as emperor of France, Napoleon established one of the largest empires in the history of the world.

The first title of the new constitution (the Constitution of the Year XII) reads as follows: "The government of the French republic is entrusted to an emperor . . . Napoleon Bonaparte, present first consul of the republic, is emperor of the French." The second title provided for the inheritance, which was to be the direct, natural, and legitimate and adoptive lineage of Napoleon. No radical innovations in the machinery of government were made. The changes in detail that the new constitution demanded completed the subjection of the legislative bodies. The Tribunate was divided into three sections and lost the right to publicly criticize the projects of the government. The Corps législatif obtained the right of discussion in secret session, but the discussions were withheld from the public unless authorized by the government. The Council of State, as before, voted decrees which the Senate issued as Consulta. The Senate itself lost whatever independence it had had, though it was given certain illusory rights which could be exercised only with the emperor's consent. A final clause provided for a plebiscite on the following proposition:

> The people desire the inheritance of the imperial dignity in the direct, natural, legitimate and adoptive lineage of Napoleon Bonaparte, and in the direct, natural, and legitimate lineage of Joseph Bonaparte and of Louis Bonaparte, as is regulated in the organic Senatus Consultum of this day.

Either Consent or Resignation

This referendum, like the preceding ones of the year VIII and the year X, implied that Napoleon would not proceed without the consent of the people, but in reality it was the seal of their resignation. It assumed their *acceptance* of the establishment of the imperial dignity and all that it submitted for their ratification was the *manner of inheritance* of the crown. As the popular vote for the empire was slightly less than that for the life consulate, Napoleon delayed publishing the figures until he had "corrected" the vote so as to show a higher total than that of 1802.

Napoleon's choice of the title "emperor" was not haphazard. He could not assume the title "king," for the Bourbon princes had not renounced their claims. Even as a legitimate king of revolutionary France, he would have placed himself in a ridiculous position. His idea was to go back to an earlier French line, to the dynasty of Charlemagne, and represent himself as the legitimate successor of the great warrior who had been emperor as well as king of the Franks. The empire was to serve as the instrument of his policy, a policy which only gradually became clear in his mind, but which even then was dimly fashioned in his thoughts. Thus the first sentence of the new constitution was highly significant, for it intimated that the empire was to be European even though the emperor ruled over the French Republic.

Having become emperor, Napoleon had to establish an imperial court and assume the ceremonies and the habits of monarchy. Invested with the imperial title, Napoleon still retained many of his old habits, but to maintain his new dignity he surrounded himself with great dignitaries, grand officers, grand marshals, and many other minor holders of titles. The second and third ex-consuls, Cambacérès and Lebrun, became arch-chancellor of the empire and arch-treasurer. His brother Joseph became grand elector, his brother Louis, constable, his brother-in-law Murat, grand admiral, and his uncle Fesch, grand almoner. Fouché received his reward in his reappointment as minister of police, a position which brought him close to the ear of the emperor. To reward Talleyrand, Napoleon was to revive the office of the old court, grand chamberlain; and his companion generals, all without exception men of the people, became grand marshals.

Haunted as he was by the name and the image of Charlemagne and anxious to impress himself upon France as the successor of the mighty Teuton, Napoleon now visited Aix-la-Chapelle, where Charlemagne's relics were buried, and he returned to Paris bearing the insignia and the sword of that ruler. Like Charlemagne, he needed the consecration of the Catholic Church; and shortly after the founding of the empire he entered into negotiations to induce Pope Pius VII to come to Paris and bestow his religious blessing at the ceremony of coronation. In the eyes of both men the matter had a political as well as a religious significance. The pope allowed himself to be convinced that the prestige of the church would be enhanced by the spectacle of the mighty emperor of the French bowing before the head of the church, and he made the arduous trip to the French capital to anoint the Corsican upstart. The coronation took place on December 2, 1804, at the cathedral of Notre Dame. No pains had been spared to make the proceedings resplendent, though a modern historian has aptly remarked, after attesting the great pomp that prevailed, that "the occasion was remarkable rather for splendor than for popular enthusiasm." It was remarkable also for its dramatic climax. As the pope was on the point of crowning the emperor, Napoleon took the crown from the hands of Pius VII and, turning his back on the venerable pontiff, faced the people and crowned himself as if to show by that gesture that he owed it to none other than himself. After crowning himself, Napoleon crowned Josephine He was now doubly consecrated; by the *vox populi* in the plebiscite and by the *vox Dei* in the religious ceremony. Of all the expectations of Pius VII, only one, and a minor one, was realized. Napoleon agreed to reëstablish the Gregorian calendar, beginning with January 1, 1806.

Reaction of Europe

It remained to be seen whether the monarchs of Europe would recognize Napoleon's title. No perspicacious statesman in Europe could fail to realize the implication of Napoleon's new dignity. [Quoted from historian E. Driault] "It was not only the consecration, almost the sanctification of the Revolution, not only a thrust to legitimacy and an offense to every established right, but a frightful threat against old monarchic Europe. . . . It was the Revolution projected forward by its own triumphant strength." From England, then at war with France, no greetings came to the new emperor. Gustavus IV, king of Sweden, scornfully referred to him as "Mister Napoleon Bonaparte." In Russia there was no question of recognizing Napoleon's new title, so strained had relations become between Alexander and Napoleon; and the sultan of Constantinople was too closely dominated by Russian influence to dare extend official recognition. On the other hand, formal letters of felicitation came promptly from the Batavian and the Italian Republics, the Helvetic Confederation Spain, and the petty German princes. The Prussian court followed suit, as did Austria, ungraciously and after several months diplomatic bargaining.

The Corsican adventurer was now emperor of the French. In four brief years he had ended "the romance of the Revolution" and established his authority over the country. He had imposed his will on France because of his practical intelligence and his soaring imagination, his boundless confidence and his tireless energy, and his genius for combining a meticulous attention to details with an undimmed vision of the ultimate object that he desired. The reorganization of France was his work. He closed the chapter of republican violence and royalist reprisal. To people sick of the Revolution he brought peace and stability without restoring the

Bourbons or sacrificing the benefits of the Revolution. He would not undo the work of the Revolution; but he could not continue it, for he was hostile to the idea of liberty which had inspired the revolutionists. For the idea of liberty he substituted the idea of authority. He retained the essentially democratic society that the Revolution had created, but he restored and perfected the centralized administration of the Old Régime. He might conceivably have ended his days as emperor of the French and perpetuated his dynasty, for the people at first welcomed his autocratic rule. But he could not pursue the safe course of peace. On more than one occasion he declared that war was essential to his political purposes; and the war which he renewed in 1803 mapped the road to his ultimate failure.

5 Beethoven's *Eroica* Symphony Is Performed: April 7, 1805

The *Eroica* Symphony Exemplified Romanticism

by Maynard Solomon

Ludwig van Beethoven, born in Germany in 1770, was one of the most talented and popular composers of all time. Beethoven's creativity is often divided into three periods reflecting different composition styles. The first period follows the late-eighteenth-century classical models established by Beethoven's predecessors. The latter period is an elaboration of Beethoven's middle period. It is this middle period (1803–1814), however, that broke from tradition and inaugurated a new musical style called romanticism. Romanticism is an early- to mid-nineteenth-century movement in art, literature, and music. Centering on themes of heroism, adventure, nature, and nationalism, romanticism celebrated both individualism and emotion.

Beethoven's *Eroica* (Heroic) symphony, the first public performance of which was in Vienna on April 7, 1805, best exemplifies his musical break from the past for two reasons. The first reason is the form incorporated into the music itself. The second involves the title of Beethoven's Third Symphony. Initially titled *Bonaparte* in honor of Napoléon, the work was eventually retitled *Eroica*. According to a popular anecdote, Beethoven changed the title because of his disdain for Napoléon's authoritarian claim to the title "emperor." As a result,

Maynard Solomon, *Beethoven*, 2nd rev. ed. New York: Schirmer Books, an imprint of Simon & Schuster Macmillan, 1998. Copyright © 1998 by Maynard Solomon. Reproduced by permission.

Beethoven later wrote on the title page of the *Eroica* that it was composed "to celebrate the memory of a great man."

The following excerpt by Maynard Solomon examines the significance of the *Eroica* Symphony both as a musical masterpiece and as a political and cultural statement. He describes the characteristics of romanticism and connects them to Beethoven's inner conflict surrounding the titling of the Third Symphony.

Maynard Solomon, a faculty member at the Juilliard School of Music, is the author of four books on Beethoven and one on Mozart.

In this symphony Beethoven had Buonaparte in mind, but as he was when he was First Consul. Beethoven esteemed him greatly at the time and likened him to the greatest Roman consuls. I as well as several of his more intimate friends saw a copy of the score lying upon his table with the word "Buonaparte" at the extreme top of the title page, and at the extreme bottom "Luigi van Beethoven," but not another word. Whether and with what the space between was to be filled out, I do not know. I was the first to bring him the intelligence that Buonaparte had proclaimed himself emperor, whereupon he flew into a rage and cried out: "Is he then, too, nothing more than an ordinary human being? Now he, too, will trample on all the rights of man and indulge only his ambition. He will exalt himself above all others, become a tyrant!" Beethoven went to the table, took hold of the title page by the top, tore it in two, and threw it on the floor. The first page was rewritten and only then did the symphony receive the title *Sinfonia eroica.*

Retitling the Symphony

This simple anecdote, told by Ferdinand Ries, is one of the more Promethean of the Beethoven legends, popular with chroniclers of romanticism and revolution. Although it describes a largely rhetorical and wholly symbolic action, it has, with the passage of time, become a monumentalized example of the artist's resistance to tyranny, of the antagonism between art and politics, of the individual against the state. But a closer examination reveals that the process by which the French leader's name was removed from Beethoven's Third Symphony was more complex than has been supposed. Furthermore, and more important, it shows that a crisis of belief was centrally involved in the crisis that precipitated and accompanied Beethoven's "new path," which he had announced . . . a few years earlier.

The accuracy of Ries's account of Beethoven's reaction to the news that Napoleon had been proclaimed emperor is not in question. Obviously, we may make allowances for Ries's rendering of Beethoven's actual words, and we know he was incorrect in saying that the symphony was thereupon or shortly thereafter retitled *Eroica*, for this name was not used before October 1806, when the first edition of the orchestral parts was published by the Bureau des Arts et d'Industrie (also called Kunstund Industrie Comtoir) in Vienna. But what Ries did not know was that in the interim Beethoven decided to restore Bonaparte's name to the symphony. On August 26, 1804, Beethoven wrote to Gottfried Härtel of [publishers] Breitkopf & Härtel:

> I have now finished several compositions . . . my oratorio—a *new grand symphony*—a concertante for violin, violoncello, and pianoforte with full orchestra—three new sonatas for pianoforte solo.
> . . . The title of the symphony is really *Bonaparte*.

Perhaps even more significant in illuminating Beethoven's indecision is the title page of his own copy of the score of the symphony. It is filled with erasures and corrections in the composer's hand. . . .

Actually, even while he was writing the symphony, Beethoven had begun to dilute his commitment to France's First Consul. Ries wrote to [music publisher Heinrich] Simrock on October 22, 1803: "He wants very much to dedicate it to Bonaparte; if not, since [patron prince] Lobkowitz wants [the rights to] it for half a year and is willing to give 400 ducats for it, he will title it Bonaparte." It seems then that Beethoven initially planned to dedicate the symphony to Bonaparte. However, finding that this would deprive him of a large fee, he conceived the alternative idea of entitling it *Bonaparte*, and it was this alternative that he confronted in May 1804 when Ries arrived, bringing the latest news from Paris. In the end, Bonaparte was to receive neither the dedication to nor the inscription of the *Eroica* Symphony.

The Napoleon Legacy

To its participants, the central issue of the post-Revolutionary age appeared to be the issue of Bonapartism, around which ideological responses to historical movements revolved. Émile Zola, in his essay on Stendhal, wrote that "Napoleon's destiny acted like a hammer-blow on the heads of his contemporaries. . . . All ambitions waxed large, all undertakings took on a gigantic air, . . . all dreams turned on universal kingship." For Beethoven's German and Austrian contemporaries, the Napoleonic image was especially potent. . . . The dramatist Franz Grillparzer wrote in his *Autobiography*, "I myself was no less an enemy of the French than my father, and yet Napoleon fascinated me with a magic power. . . . He put me under a spell, as a snake does a bird." Goethe, who kept a bust of Napoleon in his room, said to his literary assistant, Johann Peter Eckermann, in 1829, "Napoleon managed the world as Hummel his piano; both achievements appear wonderful, we do not understand one more than the other, yet so it is, and the whole is done before our eyes." Hegel, in 1806, called Napoleon a "soul of worldwide significance . . . an individual who . . . encompasses the world and rules it."

Soon, however, the difficulty of reconciling the Napoleonic ideal with the French wars of conquest—or with the Napoleonic substitution of permanent war for permanent revolution—led to confusion if not disillusionment among many European intellectuals and artists. Heinrich Heine observed that the German democrats "wrapped their thoughts in profound silence," being "too republican in their sentiments to do homage to Napoleon, and too magnanimous to ally themselves with a foreign domination." Napoleon himself noted that "everybody has loved me and hated me: everybody has taken me up, dropped me, and taken me up again. . . . I was like the sun, which crosses the equator as it describes the ecliptic; as soon as I entered each man's clime, I kindled every hope, I was blessed, I was adored; but as soon as I left it, I no longer was understood and contrary sentiments replaced the old ones."

Bonaparte's coronation was widely regarded as a subordination of principle to personal ambition. Beethoven's dismay was shared by intellectuals everywhere. [English poet Percy Bysshe] Shelley wrote, in his introduction to *The Revolt of Islam*, that "the revulsion occasioned by the atrocities of the demagogues and the reëstablishment of successive tyrannies in France was terrible, and felt in the remotest corner of the civilized world." But where Shelley optimistically continued to listen to Reason's plea for political and economic justice, and Goethe and Jefferson maintained an aloof objectivity that forbore to take sides on issues where morality was unable to choose, others, such as Coleridge and Wordsworth, became obsessed with fears of the Jacobin danger and opted for a restoration of the ancien régime. For his part, Beethoven neither gave way to spiritual melancholia over this issue nor abandoned his belief in the secular, fraternal utopia that Bonaparte—one *bon prince*—had betrayed.

Beethoven's Attitude

The Revolution was over, dissolved in war and petrified in the stultifying bureaucratic forms that sooner or later overtake all social transformations. But this was a process that had begun well before 1804. Beethoven's rending of the title page therefore cannot be accepted as a simple act of angry defiance at a new development in Napoleonic politics, for these regressive tendencies had already been apparent for some years, and Beethoven was aware of them. His equivocal attitude toward the French leader neither started nor ended with the Imperium. Beethoven's composition of two patriotic songs in 1796 and 1797 was inspired by Habsburg anti-Napoleonic campaigns, and Beethoven had even explicitly expressed his disillusionment with Napoleon in 1802, when Hoffmeister, the Leipzig publisher, transmitted a suggestion that Beethoven compose a sonata in celebration of Napoleon or of the Revolution. Beethoven's reply to Hoffmeister of April 8, 1802, indicates that even then—shortly before the *Eroica* Symphony was begun—he considered Bonaparte to have betrayed the Revolution by virtue of his concordat with the Vatican (signed in July 1801), which reestablished Catholic worship in France:

> Has the devil got hold of you all, Gentlemen?—that you suggest that *I should compose such a sonata.* Well, perhaps at the time of the *Revolutionary* fever—such a thing might have been possible, but now, when everything is trying to slip back into the old rut, now that *Buonaparte* has concluded his *Concordat* with the Pope—to write a sonata of that kind? . . . But good Heavens, such a sonata— in these newly developing Christian times—Ho ho—there you must leave me out—you won't get anything from me—.

Why, then, did Beethoven decide to write a *Bonaparte* symphony shortly after this letter to Hoffmeister? . . .

The Significance of Dedications

Beethoven was emerging from what seemed to be a period of ideological quiescence. Perhaps this is one reason why, in the opening years of the nineteenth century, he began a series of apparently disinterested dedications of his works to leading exponents of enlightened views. Thus, in December 1801 he inscribed his Symphony No. 1 in C, op. 21, to Baron Gottfried van Swieten, reformer, presumed Freemason, and a guardian to Mozart's orphaned sons; next, the revered Austrian-Jewish *Aufklärer*, Freemason, and Illuminist Joseph von Sonnenfels (favorite of and adviser to Emperor Joseph II) received the dedication of the Piano Sonata in D, op. 28, in August 1802; and the young Czar Alexander, who had instituted a program of reform in the tradition of Enlightened despotism, received that of the three Sonatas for Violin and Piano, op. 30, in 1803. Because dedications for Beethoven were either a major source of patronage and income or a means of expressing gratitude or friendship, these unpaid, honorary dedications are all the more significant.

The culmination of this series was the proposed dedication to Bonaparte of the Third Symphony. This dedication, along with the consideration of a move to Paris, may, therefore, have been a dramatic sign of Beethoven's desire to break with Habsburg Vienna and its political system as well as with its modes of musical patronage. If this is true, then the rending of the inscription may constitute an equally dramatic turning point—Beethoven's abandonment of his identification with France and his decision henceforth to view himself as a citizen of Vienna.

The idea of a symphonic apotheosis of Napoleon had been worked out during the relatively long period of peace that followed Napoleon's defeat of Austria in late 1800, as codified by the February 9, 1801, Treaty of Lunéville. That peace was unraveling in 1804, and war was to erupt once again in 1805. To have kept "Bonaparte" either as title or as dedication at a moment when renewed war between France and Austria was imminent would have marked Beethoven as a philo-Jacobin, a supporter of a radical cause and of a hostile power. It would have led not merely to the loss of a patron—Lobkowitz was an ardent patriot who later raised a battalion of troops to fight the French—but to the probability of reprisals in anti-Revolutionary Austria as well.

Of all the European nations, writes Eric Hobsbawm, "Austria, whose family links with the Bourbons were reinforced by the direct French threat to her possessions and areas of influence in Italy, and her leading position in Germany, was the most consistently anti-French, and took part in every major coalition against

France." Austria suffered heavier defeats and territorial losses than any other continental power during the Napoleonic Wars. We saw earlier how the Viennese authorities kept constant watch on all expression of social or political dissent. And of all forms of dissent, support for France was considered the most dangerous.

In light of these circumstances, Beethoven's obliteration of the Bonaparte inscription and the consequent merging of his heroic ideal with the Habsburg national outlook can be seen as his passport to Viennese citizenship. . . .

A Deeper Meaning

From May 13 to November 20, 1809, Vienna was occupied by the French. Napoleon's eagle perched on the masthead of the *Wiener Zeitung*; a cantata, *Sieg der Eintracht*, was written by Ignaz Castelli and Joseph Weigl to celebrate the marriage of Napoleon to the Habsburg princess Maria Louise; the best artists of Vienna were called to Schönbrunn to perform for Bonaparte. Beethoven was not called. On September 8, he conducted his *Eroica* Symphony at a charity concert at the Theater-an-der-Wien for the theatrical poor fund (*Theaterarmen*). [Biographer Alexander] Thayer asks, "Was this selected, in the expectation that Napoleon would be present, to do him homage? If so it failed of its aim. The day before, Napoleon journeyed from Schönbrunn. . . . Or was it in bitter sarcasm that Beethoven chose it?" The latter possibility is unlikely, for Max Unger has turned up Beethoven's extraordinary note to himself of October 8, 1810: "The Mass [in C, op. 86] could perhaps be dedicated to Napoleon." It is a pity that we have only the insufficient word "ambivalence" to describe such total reversals of emotional attitude—surely too tame a word for so turbulent a set of feelings. What is involved, actually, is not merely a series of reversals but an insoluble conflict that can be resolved, if at all, only through a change in the balance of forces. This was to come later, with Napoleon's defeat at Waterloo, his exile to St. Helena, and his death.

But even after those events it is doubtful that Beethoven ever came to terms with Bonaparte. On hearing of Napoleon's death on May 5, 1821, Beethoven remarked, rather enigmatically, "I have already composed the proper music for that catastrophe"; and in 1824 he said to Czerny, "Napoleon, I could not tolerate him earlier. Now I think quite differently."

Perhaps it is in Beethoven's ambivalence itself that we have a

clue to a deeper meaning of Bonaparte's connection with the
Eroica. As we have seen, it is a curious fact that there is no evidence whatever that Beethoven had anything other than negative
feelings toward Bonaparte prior to 1803. His reported brief association with the French ambassador [Jean Baptiste] Bernadotte in
1798 does not contradict this, for Bernadotte was himself on extremely bad terms with Bonaparte. ([Anton] Schindler, who mis-
takenly believed that Bernadotte was still ambassador in 1804,
thus was probably equally mistaken in claiming that Bernadotte
suggested that Beethoven write a composition in honor of Bonaparte.) The *Eroica* Symphony, therefore, may not, after all, have
been conceived in a spirit of homage, which was then superseded
by disillusionment. Rather, it is possible that Beethoven chose as
his subject one toward whom he already felt an unconquerable
ambivalence containing a strong component of hostility. The symphony, with its Funeral March movement, is centrally concerned
with the death of the hero as well as with his birth and resurrec-
tion: "Composed," Beethoven eventually wrote on the title page,
"to celebrate the memory of a great man." Striving to free himself
from his lifelong pattern of submission to the domination of authority figures, Beethoven was drawn to the conqueror who had
confounded the venerable leaders of Europe and set himself in
their place. If homage is on the surface, the underlying themes are
patricide and fratricide, mingled with the survivor's sense of triumph. As in the "Joseph" Cantata, piety toward the departed hero
may mask feelings of an opposite kind.

According to one of his physicians, Joseph Bertolini, Beethoven's
original plan had been to compose the Funeral March of the
Eroica on a British topic, either the wounding of Lord Nelson at
the Battle of the Nile in 1798 or the death of General Ralph Abercromby at Alexandria in 1801. In view of Beethoven's steadfast
admiration for the British (which dated back to his family's friendship with George Cressener, the British ambassador to Bonn), Nelson or Abercromby could not serve as appropriate subjects of the
conflicting emotions that are condensed in the *Eroica*. And so
Beethoven may have fixed upon one toward whom he had mixed
feelings, one whom he had already rejected as an ideal prince/leg-
islator. Thus, the choice of Bonaparte as his subject and the rending of the inscription may have been part of the same process: of
establishing parity with and hegemony over the most powerful figure of the era. Beethoven disposed of Bonaparte twice—once in

composing the symphony and again in removing his name from the title.

Heroism of the *Eroica*

Georg Brandes described German romanticism's glorification of desire, of wish, as "impotence itself conceived as a power." A sense of national impotence lay just behind the facade of Viennese life after the death of Joseph II, with whom were interred the thwarted hopes for Enlightened absolutism. These feelings of futility were reinforced by the Habsburgs' abject submission to Napoleon following the succession of crushing military defeats between 1797 and 1809.

That Beethoven was capable of producing the ultimate musical definition of heroism in this context is itself extraordinary, for he was able to evoke a dream heroism that neither he nor his native Germany nor his adopted Vienna could express in reality. Perhaps we can only measure the heroism of the *Eroica* by the depths of fear and uncertainty from which it emerged.

There was a component of caution, an excess of discretion, even a failure of nerve, in Beethoven's removal of the Bonaparte inscription. This should not, however, lead us to reject other levels of motivation and meaning. As we have seen, Beethoven regarded Bonaparte as an embodiment of Enlightened leadership, but, simultaneously, he felt betrayed by Bonaparte's Caesarist deeds. Beethoven's ambivalence mirrored a central contradiction of his age, and it is this contradiction that finds expression in the *Eroica* Symphony. The *Eroica* arose from the conflict between Enlightened faith in the savior-prince and the reality of Bonapartism. Bonaparte— whose image replaced Christ's in myriads of European homes—had inherited the displaced messianism of his time; Beethoven, who rejected blind faith and hierarchical orthodoxy in his personal theology, now rejected its secular equivalents. As an artist and a man, Beethoven could no longer accept unmediated conceptions of progress, innate human goodness, reason, and faith. His affirmations were now leavened by an acknowledgment of the frailty of human leadership and a consciousness of the regressive and brutalizing components in all forward-thrusting stages in social evolution.

Faith and Skepticism

Beethoven, ever questioning, spurred by doubt, rejecting the passivity of superstition and the false confidence of ideological certainty, never abandoned his central faith in the values of the Enlightenment—altruistic love, reason, and humanistic ideals. The Enlightenment abjured superstition and dogma and supplanted theological pessimism about the possibilities of earthly salvation with a harmonious and optimistic view of mankind's freedom to develop its potentialities within a framework of natural law and political reconstruction. This is not to say that its philosophers were unaware of the problem of evil or that its views were predicated upon a banal rejection of skepticism. Nevertheless, as Ernst Cassirer observed, "This era is permeated by genuine creative feeling and an unquestionable faith in the reformation of the world"; and he quoted Voltaire's maxim "*Some day all will be well,* is our hope; *all is well today,* is illusion." Beethoven rejected the latter illusion, and cleaved to the principle of hope.

Beethoven could not have "journeyed to Paris," which is to say, transferred his allegiance to France, without becoming a musical conformist working in conventional formulas. . . . French Revolutionary music (and painting) largely ignored both the Revolution and the Terror, stressing instead nobility of motivation and action and substituting heroic portraiture and triumphal rhetoric for conflict and tragedy. Idealism and simple faith alone, however, are insufficient grounds for greatness. Conflict is absent from such ideological formulations, and the artworks that result accordingly require no formal containment, but merely craftsmanlike expression. For it is the conflict between faith and skepticism, the struggle between belief and disbelief—which Goethe described as the most important theme of world history—that creates those dynamic tensions that tend to expand and threaten to burst the bonds of form. The *Eroica* Symphony is Beethoven's elaboration of that theme in the closing hours of the Enlightenment.

Beethoven's *Eroica* Symphony Is Performed:
April 7, 1805

Art Is What Saved Me

by Ludwig van Beethoven

In addition to being a creative compositional genius, Ludwig van Beethoven was also a virtuoso pianist early in his career. His days as a performer came to an unfortunate end, though, when he became afflicted with deafness around 1800. Although he suffered bouts of deafness and related hearing impairment for many years, Beethoven was totally deaf for approximately the last ten years of his life (1817–1827).

Beethoven's deafness was overwhelmingly frustrating for him from the very beginning, so much so that on October 6, 1802, he penned a document titled the "Heiligenstadt Testament." Addressed to his brothers, the letter (which was never sent) captures Beethoven's physical and emotional distress as he copes with the effects of his illness at the age of thirty-one. Written while Beethoven was on a restful retreat in Heiligenstadt, Austria, the testament reveals despair so pervasive that the composer did not think he would survive the winter. Out of this despair, however, emerged a new realm of creativity. The first major product of this triumphant creativity was Beethoven's Third Symphony, the *Eroica* (Heroic). This symphony represents a transition from the classical tradition to the spirited, emotional qualities of what was to become the "romanticism" movement. Beethoven began writing it in 1802 and completed it in 1804. The *Eroica* was performed, with Beethoven as the conductor, for the first time in Vienna on April 7, 1805.

Ludwig van Beethoven, "Letter to Brothers Carl and Johann," *Beethoven's Letters (1790–1826) from the Collection of Ludwig Nohl*, translated by Lady Wallace. Boston: Longwood Press, 1978.

To MY BROTHERS CARL AND JOHANN BEETHOVEN.

Heiligenstadt, Oct. 6, 1802.

Oh! ye who think or declare me to be hostile, morose, and misanthropical, how unjust you are, and how little you know the secret cause of what appears thus to you! My heart and mind were ever from childhood prone to the most tender feelings of affection, and I was always disposed to accomplish something great. But you must remember that six years ago I was attacked by an incurable malady, aggravated by unskillful physicians, deluded from year to year, too, by the hope of relief, and at length forced to the conviction of a *lasting affliction* (the cure of which may go on for years, and perhaps after all prove impracticable).

Deafness and Isolation

Born with a passionate and excitable temperament, keenly susceptible to the pleasures of society, I was yet obliged early in life to isolate myself, and to pass my existence in solitude. If I at any time resolved to surmount all this, oh! how cruelly was I again repelled by the experience, sadder than ever, of my defective hearing!—and yet I found it impossible to say to others: Speak louder; shout! for I am deaf! Alas! how could I proclaim the deficiency of a sense which ought to have been more perfect with me than with other men,—a sense which I once possessed in the highest perfection, to an extent, indeed, that few of my profession ever enjoyed! Alas, I cannot do this! Forgive me therefore when you see me withdraw from you with whom I would so gladly mingle. My misfortune is doubly severe from causing me to be misunderstood. No longer can I enjoy recreation in social intercourse, refined conversation, or mutual outpourings of thought. Completely isolated, I only enter society when compelled to do so. I must live like an exile. In company I am assailed by the most painful apprehensions, from the dread of being exposed to the risk of my condition being observed. It was the same during the last six months I spent in the country. My intelligent physician recommended me to spare my hearing as much as possible, which was quite in accordance with my present disposition, though sometimes, tempted by my natural inclination for society, I allowed myself to be beguiled into it. But what humiliation when any one beside me heard a flute in the far distance, while I heard *nothing*, or when others heard *a shepherd singing*, and I still heard *nothing!*

Art Deterred Me

Such things brought me to the verge of desperation, and wellnigh caused me to put an end to my life. *Art! art* alone, deterred me. Ah! how could I possibly quit the world before bringing forth all that I felt it was my vocation to produce? And thus I spared this miserable life—so utterly miserable that any sudden change may reduce me at any moment from my best condition into the worst. It is decreed that I must now choose *Patience* for my guide! This I have done. I hope the resolve will not fail me, steadfastly to persevere till it may please the inexorable Fates to cut the thread of my life. Perhaps I may get better, perhaps not. I am prepared for either. Constrained to become a philosopher in my twenty-eighth year! This is no slight trial, and more severe on an artist than on any one else. God looks into my heart, He searches it, and knows that love for

Ludwig van Beethoven

man and feelings of benevolence have their abode there! Oh! ye who may one day read this, think that you have done me injustice, and let any one similarly afflicted be consoled, by finding one like himself, who, in defiance of all the obstacles of Nature, has done all in his power to be included in the ranks of estimable artists and men. My brothers Carl and Johann, as soon as I am no more, if Professor Schmidt be still alive, beg him in my name to describe my malady, and to add these pages to the analysis of my disease, that at least, so far as possible, the world may be reconciled to me after my death.

Virtue Sustains Happiness

I also hereby declare you both heirs of my small fortune (if so it may be called). Share it fairly, agree together and assist each other. You know that anything you did to give me pain has been long forgiven. I thank you, my brother Carl in particular, for the attachment you have shown me of late. My wish is that you may enjoy a happier life, and one more free from care, than mine has been. Recommend *Virtue* to your children; that alone, and not wealth, can ensure happiness. I speak from experience. It was *Virtue* alone which sustained me in my misery; I have to thank her and Art for not having ended my life by suicide. Farewell! Love each other. I gratefully thank all my friends, especially Prince Lichnowsky and Professor Schmidt. I wish one of you to keep Prince L——'s instruments; but I trust this will give rise to no dissension between you. If you think it more beneficial, however, you have only to dispose of them. How much I shall rejoice if I can serve you even in the grave! So be it then! I joyfully hasten to meet Death. If he comes before I have had the opportunity of developing all my artistic powers, then, notwithstanding my cruel fate, he will come too early for me, and I should wish for him at a more distant period; but even then I shall be content, for his advent will release me from a state of endless suffering. Come when he may, I shall meet him with courage. Farewell! Do not quite forget me, even in death; I deserve this from you, because during my life I so often thought of you, and wished to make you happy. Amen!

(Written on the Outside.)

THUS, then, I take leave of you, and with sadness too. The fond hope I brought with me here, of being to a certain degree cured, now utterly forsakes me. As autumn leaves fall and wither, so are my hopes blighted. Almost as I came, I depart. Even the lofty courage that so often animated me in the lovely days of summer is gone forever. O Providence! vouchsafe me one day of pure felicity! How long have I been estranged from the glad echo of true joy! When! O my God! when shall I again feel it in the temple of Nature and of man?—never? Ah! that would be too hard!

(Outside.)

To be read and fulfilled after my death by my brothers Carl and Johann.

**Lewis and Clark Return from Their Expedition:
September 23, 1806**

Lewis and Clark Complete the First Transcontinental Exploration

by John Logan Allen

The Louisiana Purchase of 1803, which nearly doubled the size of the United States, consisted of territory mostly unfamiliar to Americans. For this reason, President Thomas Jefferson asked Congress for twenty-five hundred dollars to fund an organized exploration. Meriwether Lewis, a former soldier and Jefferson's private secretary, was appointed commander of the expedition. He selected former soldier and skilled mapmaker William Clark to help him lead the exploration. Lewis and Clark, together with the band of thirty-plus men who accompanied them on the journey, formed the Corps of Discovery.

The Lewis and Clark expedition, which covered over eight thousand miles, lasted from May 14, 1804, to September 23, 1806. The exploration went from the Missouri River to the Rocky Mountains, and then downstream to the Pacific Ocean. Over the course of twenty-eight months, only one man from the exploration party died. During this time, the explorers also had numerous encounters with Native Americans. All but one of these encounters were amiable; overall, the explorers were grateful to the Native Americans for continuously providing helpful guidance through unknown lands.

The following selection by John Logan Allen describes the mys-

John Logan Allen, *Passage Through the Garden: Lewis and Clark and the Image of the American Northwest*. Chicago: University of Illinois Press, 1975. Copyright © 1975 by John Logan Allen. Reproduced by permission.

tery of the unknown territory of the Louisiana Purchase. The unfamiliar region is often referred to as the Northwest Passage because of a (futile) hope for a navigable water route that would be a "passage" from the Atlantic to the Pacific. Allen explains Americans' perception of northwestern geography and why the West had so much appeal.

John Logan Allen is a professor and chair of the department of geography and recreation at the University of Wyoming. His research and publications focus on exploration and the human impact on nature.

T he European colonial powers had sought a way through the continent of North America, and the United States was also interested in the Passage to India. But her motives were just as political and territorial as they were commercial, and her people viewed the West in the light of their 200-year heritage of hewing homes from the wilderness. While the European explorers had sought the ephemeral passage to the Orient, Americans had been, as Thoreau said, "realizing westward." By the beginning of the nineteenth century, as European exploration below the 50th parallel trickled to an end and as the mists rolled in across the great river Missouri, across the wild grape and briar and sod, across the fields of corn and squash and the earthen lodges of the Mandan and Hidatsa [Native American] nations, the vanguard of American expansion had reached the edge of the Northwest.

The Northwestern Mystery

The standard bearers of the American folk migration looked into the West and saw not only the future possibilities of the commercial passage to the Pacific that had concerned Europeans and Americans alike for so many generations. They saw also, mingled with optimism and desire and longing, the vision of "one happy union, the whole country from the Atlantic to the Pacific Ocean, and from the lakes of Canada to the Gulf of Mexico." The poets would record the vision:

Towards the desert turn our anxious eyes,
To see 'mong forest statelier cities rise;
Where the wild beast now holds his gloomy den,
To see shine forth the blessed abodes of men.

The rich luxuriance of a teeming soil,
Rewards with affluence the farmer's toil,
All nature round him breathes a rich perfume,
His harvest ripens and his orchards bloom.

The water route to the Pacific was, for many Americans, a Passage through the Garden. That fact lent zest and flavor to early nineteenth-century American images of the Northwest, images out of which grew the grand designs of Jefferson and his contemporaries to unravel the Northwestern Mystery.

The United States in the new nineteenth century was an agricultural nation. Thomas Jefferson, who considered the independent small farmer the backbone of an ideal republic, had been elected president in the disputed election of 1800 partly because of his adherence to the agrarian tradition. It is only natural, perhaps, that American images of the Northwest should have been colored by the predominant feeling that the United States had to maintain vast areas for the expansion of an agricultural population if she were to remain a republic. The dominant portion of the Americans' images of the Northwest, in terms of land quality, could only have been based on hope and optimism—a hope that the lands to the west would provide a firm base for the agrarian republic and an optimism that this must be the case.

Detractors might have written in the newspapers of the larger cities of the seaboard that the West was "an absolute barren that nobody knows the bounds of or cares." Indeed, many of the reports of the later Spanish-sponsored explorers such as Truteau might have (insofar as these reports were available) substantiated this notion. But these critics were not in the majority. The Northwest was, of course, a large area with room for lands of both high and low quality. But the majority of the source materials available to Americans spoke of fertility and lushness, and the revelations were widely accepted. It mattered little that the source materials were describing only the fecundity of the Mississippi valley and its immediately adjacent area. For when information on an entire region is limited, regional differences and distinctions within that area are blurred in the images that are created for it. Data on one part of a region, if it is the only information available, becomes applied to the region as a whole. Because the greatest volume of lore that Americans possessed about the Northwest depicted it as a garden, a garden it was in the mind's eye of the early nineteenth century, full of hopes and not disillusionment.

Knowledge and Myth

Like the view of the land itself, the ideas on what the land contained were based on the agrarian tradition. For centuries wealth in gold, gems, and precious minerals had been sought toward the sunset, but in the American images of the Northwest in the early nineteenth century few elements of El Dorado remained. The official reports of government investigations might have set forth the notion that the lands of the trans-Missouri region contained precious minerals locked in their bowels, but the traditional emphasis on mineral wealth was more practical. To most Americans who thought about the Northwest and the future potential of the region, lead, iron, and salt—the basic needs of a frontier agricultural society—were foremost; gold, silver, and other precious metals could come later.

If optimism cloaked the American images of the Northwest with regard to the quality of the land and the salubrity of the climate, so also did it permeate the nature of American thought about the native inhabitants of that area. Correspondents writing from the borderlands of the Mississippi to eastern papers had posted the news that not only was the Northwest the land of promise, with soils of great fertility and hordes of grazing beasts, but also that there were "no hostile Indians to contend with." Few Americans had come in contact with the Plains tribes (the French and Spanish fur traders, who had, would have told a different story), and, although they should have known better, Americans tended to view the western Indians as distinct from the eastern tribes.

Like other features of the Northwest, the natives were surrounded with an aura of mystery. They were somehow different and more romantic than the general run-of-the-mill Indians. Some authorities thought it highly probable that many of the western tribes were descended from various pre-Columbian European adventurers such as the Irish, the Norse, or even the Welsh. Or perhaps the western natives were remnants of the Lost Tribes of Israel. Some of them were white and some of them were black and some of them wore beards and lived in cities of gold in conditions which approached and rivaled (if not excelled) the standards of European civilizations. The farther west one went the more likely he would be to encounter utopian civilizations and fabulous peoples. This was a function of a general tendency to fill the least-known areas on a map with the least likely phenomena. It was also a function of the romanticism inherent in geographical thought about the lands toward the sunset.

In spite of these tendencies toward romantic and image-filled attitudes about the Northwest, the American views of the region contained surprisingly little of a mythical character. Many of the geographical elements of the Northwest were poorly understood; but there were few true features of myth in the components of western geography. Concepts of land fertility, notions about the size and height and location of interior mountains, theoretical ideas about symmetrical drainage patterns and common source areas for major rivers—these all had some basis in fact that was misconstrued and misunderstood. It is true that some literature of the early 1800s contained wild tales about great lakes in the interior, surrounded by civilized natives living in splendid cities. And other literary sources discussed the possibilities of discovering beasts of medieval mythic character in the mountains and plains of the Northwest. But such fanciful imaginings do not seem to have been a part of general geographical lore.

Of all the features of the geography of the Northwest that might be considered mythical, only two gained any measure of popular acceptance. The first of these was a mountain of rock salt, described in articles in the most reputable periodicals and geographical writings. After the cession of Louisiana to the United States in 1803, even the government's official account of the lands encompassed in the newly acquired territory reported solemnly that there was, about a thousand miles up the Missouri, a mountain of solid rock salt, 180 miles long and 45 wide, without a single stick of vegetation on it. A second popular notion dealt with the presence of great volcanoes in the interior. Travelers who had been on the Missouri had seen and brought back pieces of pumice stone found floating on the waters of the river. These were considered to have been produced by volcanic activity and proved conclusively the existence of lofty volcanoes in, as a major scientific periodical had it, "those immense and unexplored mountains which may be called 'the Northern Andes.'" Beyond the widespread acceptance of these two fictions there seems to have been little else in the American images that was without some basis in fact.

The absence of mythical features in the literature and lore of the years just before Lewis and Clark notwithstanding, it must be noted that Americans had already developed the propensity to "talk tall." But this tendency meant other things than the creation of a mythical geography for the interior; rather than filling the empty spaces on the map with pure fantasy, Americans chose to exaggerate what they had learned about the Northwest from the accounts and chronicles of the seventeenth and eighteenth centuries. The soils of the West were the best in the world, the climate was gentle and kind, and the natives resembled heroic races of Homeric proportions. The West was a land of opportunity—even at this early date—and should be viewed with optimism and hope. It would provide the home for the expansion of the republic and through its vast river systems, connecting with short portages through mountains that were no barriers to the spread of American civilization, that republic might reach the Pacific and the Orient beyond. . . .

Interpreting Information

If knowledge could be envisioned as three-dimensional, then the general American lore on the trans-Missouri region on the eve of Lewis's and Clark's trek could best be described as a basin, surrounded by ridges of better knowledge and grading into a vast, flat surface of pure conjecture, broken here and there by a peak of better understanding. Exploratory approaches had been made to the Northwest from several sides, and as a result of these approaches the periphery of the area was relatively well known. The American view of the lower portions of the Missouri and of the Pacific coastal area near the mouth of the Columbia was fairly accurate, derived from the coastal surveys of the British in the Pacific Northwest and from the long-term French and Spanish contacts in the lower Missouri valley. But these well-known areas graded into others, such as the portion of the Missouri from the mouth of the Kansas to the Mandan villages, that were known only partially through the brief contacts of the fur traders of Spanish Louisiana. Beyond this lay only rumor and conjecture, and perhaps the single most striking feature of American geographical knowledge of the Northwest before Lewis and Clark was the almost total lack of good information on the western interior.

But lack of information does not curtail the ability to create images, and in spite of poor and inadequate data on western geography there were definite patterns of belief in the nature and content of the geographical features of the Northwest in the minds of many Americans. These images were based on American interpretations of the knowledge contributed by exploration in the trans-Missouri area from Marquette to Mackay and Evans, and in the American view appeared the twin themes of the Garden of the World and the Passage to India. Because of the confused and contradictory nature of American geographical lore, however, the images and the themes were blurred. Still, a clear image would come out of the chaos.

There were, in the opening years of the nineteenth century, some Americans who were possessed of better information and more complete understanding of the Northwest than most of their contemporaries. Through the articulation of the fuzzier and less specific overall American images by these individuals a plan of action was laid out. From that plan of action would come the first American expedition into the trans-Missouri area, and that expedition would begin to burn off the mists and begin to light the darkness that had cloaked the American Northwest. This was the expedition of Lewis and Clark, the product of the distillation and refinement of the American views of the lands lying between the Mississippi and the Pacific.

The Role of Thomas Jefferson

The journey of Lewis and Clark to the great South Sea and back was aided, furthered, and made feasible by soldiers, frontier civilians, scientists, and government officials. But perhaps more than any other event in the history of exploration it was generated by the geographical understanding and imagination of one man. Towering above all other contributors to the success of the Lewis and Clark Expedition was Thomas Jefferson. It was through his formulation and implementation of the images of the Northwest that the first American transcontinental exploration became a reality. Like others of his time, Jefferson saw a garden in the Northwest, and a basic part of his desire to have the region explored was to establish firmly and scientifically that the country beyond the Mississippi was, in truth, eminently suited for occupation by the agrarian society. But another idea was even more central in Jeffersons' thinking—through the Garden lay the Passage to India. . . .

The allure of the Passage to India . . . never left Jefferson. Throughout most of his mature life he gathered materials that would provide him with information about that transcontinental communication. From that information on the history, exploration, and geography of the western parts of North America there developed an image of the Northwest, an image that contained not only the element of the Passage to India but also many other elements that had emerged from the exploratory experiences of the French, British, and Spanish from 1673 to the cession of Louisiana to the United States.

Encounters and Obstacles on the Expedition

by Meriwether Lewis and William Clark

Meriwether Lewis and William Clark began their exploration of the American Northwest in St. Louis, Missouri. The expedition team, known as the Corps of Discovery, proceeded to present-day North Dakota, where they settled for the winter. They were then aided by Sacajawea, a woman of the Shoshone tribe, in their quest to explore the Rocky Mountains. The trek continued to the Pacific Ocean, from which point the explorers retraced their steps, parted briefly, and joined again to return home on September 23, 1806.

Lewis, Clark, and many members of their team recorded their thoughts and experiences in notes, journals, and drawings. They collected natural specimens and Native American artifacts. The expedition gathered information not only about the geography of the Louisiana Purchase but also about the area's inhabitants.

The following are journal excerpts by Lewis and Clark from June 14 to June 20, 1806, just a few months before the conclusion of their journey. At the time of these writings, the expedition was re-crossing the Rocky Mountains. Both Lewis and Clark describe the challenging weather conditions and the obstacles they encountered as a result. The journal excerpts provide insight into the decisions Lewis and Clark made regarding the route and their short-range excursion plans.

Meriwether Lewis and William Clark, "The Journals," *Lewis & Clark, PBS Online*, www.pbs.org.

June 12, 1806
William Clark
we made a digest of the Indian Nations West of the Rocky Mountains which we have seen and of whom we have been repeatedly informed by those with whom we were conversent. they amount by our estimate to 69.000 (about 80,000) Souls.

Snow Causes a Delay

June 14, 1806
Meriwether Lewis
from hence to traveller's rest we shall make a forsed march; at that place we shal probably remain one or two days to rest ourselves and horses and procure some meat. we have now been detained near five weeks in consequence of the snows; a serious loss of time at this delightfull season for traveling. I am still apprehensive that the snow and the want of food for our horses will prove a serious imbarrassment to us as at least four days journey of our rout in these mountains lies over hights and along a ledge of mountains never intirely destitute of snow. every body seems anxious to be in motion, convinced that we have not now any time to delay if the calculation is to reach the United States this season; this I am detirmined to accomplish if within the compass of human power.

June 14, 1806
William Clark
we expect to set out early, and shall proceed with as much expedition as possible over those snowey tremendious mountains which has detained us near five weeks in this neighbourhood waiting for the Snows to melt sufficient for us to pass over them. and even now I shudder with the expectation with [of] great dificuelties in passing those Mountains, from the debth of snow and the want of grass sufficient to subsist our horses, . . .

June 15, 1806
Meriwether Lewis
it rained very hard in the morning . . . Came 22 Miles today.

June 16, 1806
Meriwether Lewis
We collected our horses very readily this morning, took break-

fast and set out at 6 A.M.; . . . we arrived at a small branch of hungry creek. . . . this morning Windsor busted his rifle near the muzzle. . . . large quantities of snow yet undesolved; in some places it was from two to three feet deep. . . . the snow has increased in quantity so much that the greater part of our rout this evening was over the snow which has become sufficiently firm to bear our horshes, otherwise it would have been impossible for us to proceed as it lay in immence masses in some places 8 or ten feet deep. . . . the air is pleasent in the course of the day but becomes very cold before morning notwitstanding the shortness of the nights. . . . the water is perfectly transparent and as cold as ice. . . . we came 15 miles today.

June 16, 1806
    William Clark
    We found much difficulty in finding the road, as it was so frequently covered with snow.

Compelled to Retreat

June 17, 1806
    Meriwether Lewis
    . . . we found ourselves invelloped in snow from 12 to 15 feet deep even on the south sides of the hills with the fairest exposure to the sun; here was winter with all it's rigors; the air was cold, my hands and feet were benumbed. . . . if we proceeded and should get bewildered in these mountains the certainty was that we should loose all our horses and consequently our baggage inst[r]uments perhaps our papers and thus eminently wrisk the loss of the discoveries which we had already made if we should be so fortunate as to escape with life. . . . under these circumstances we conceived it madness in this stage of the expedition to proceed without a guide who could certainly conduct us to the fish wears on the Kooskooske, as our horses could not possibly sustain a journey of more than five days without food. we therefore came to the resolution to return with our horses while they were yet strong and in good order and indevour to keep them so untill we could procure an indian to conduct us over the snowey mountains, and again to proceed as soon as we could procure such a guide, . . . we ordered the party to make a deposit for all the baggage which we had not immediate use for, and also all the roots and bread of cows which they had except an allowance for a few days to enable them to re-

turn to some place at which we could subsist by hunting untill we procured a guide. we left our instruments papers &c. beleiving them safer here than to wrisk them on horseback over the roads and creeks which we had passed. our baggage being laid on scaffoalds . . . we returned by the rout we had come to hungry creek, . . . the party were a good deel dejected tho' not as much so as I had apprehended they would have been. this is the first time since we have been on this long tour that we have ever been compelled to retreat or make a retrograde march. it rained on us most of this evening.

June 17, 1806
William Clark
. . . I with great difficulty prosued the direction of the road one mile further to the top of the mountain where I found the snow from 12 to 15 feet deep, but fiew trees with the fairest exposure to the Sun; here was Winter with all it's rigors; the air was cold my hands and feet were benumed. . . . the snow bore our horses very well and the traveling was therefore infinately better than the obstruction of rocks and fallen timber which we met with in our passage over last fall when the snow lay on this part of the ridge in detached spots only. . . . on the top of the Mountain the Weather was very fluctiating and uncertain snowed cloudy & fair in a few minets.

The Hunters Have No Success

June 18, 1806
Meriwether Lewis
We dispatched Drewyer and Shannon to the Chopunnish Indians in the plains . . . we sent by them a rifle which we offered as a reward to any of them who would engage to conduct us to traveller's rest: we also dirrected them if they found difficulty in inducing any of them to accompany us to offer the reward of two other guns to be given them immediately and ten horses at the falls of Missouri. . . . Potts cut his leg very badly with one of the large knives; . . . Colter's horse fell with him in passing hungry creek and himself and horse were driven down the creek a considerable distance rolling over each other among the rocks. fortunately [he] escaped without injury . . . we sent out several hunters but they returned without having killed anything. they saw a number of salmon (trout) in the creek and shot at them several times without success. . . . we hope by means of the fish together with what deer and bear we can kill to be enabled to subsist untill our guide ar-

rives without the necessity of returning to the quawmash [a root plant] flats.

June 18, 1806
    William Clark
    Colters horse fell with him in passing hungary creek . . . he lost his blanket. Musquetors Troublesome.

June 19, 1806
    Meriwether Lewis
    the Fishermen had been more unsuccessfull, they returned without a single fish and reported that they could find but few and those they had tryed to take in vain. they had broke both their giggs which were of indian fabrication made of bone. . . . they took one fish this evening which proved to be salmon trout much to our mortification, . . . we determined to send out all the hunters in the morning in order to make a fair experiment of the p[r]act[ica]bility of our being able to subsist at this place and if not we shall move the day after to the Quawmash flatts. . . . Cruzatte brought me several large morells which I roasted and eat without salt pepper or grease in this way I had for the first time the true taist of the morell which is truly an insippid taistless food. our stock of salt is now exhausted except two quarts which I have reserved for my tour up Maria's River and that I left the other day on the mountain.

June 19, 1806
    William Clark
    (Food for horses, but not men. . . .)
    . . . I observed a great abundance of fine grass sufficient to sustain our horses any length of time we chose to stay at this place. . . . should we get a guide from this place it will save us two days march through some of the worst road through those Mountains, crouded with fallin timber mudholes and steep hills &c. we directed all the hunters to turn out early and kill something for us to live on &c.

Planning the Next Route

June 20, 1806
    Meriwether Lewis
    the hunters assured us that their greatest exertions would not enable them to support us here more than one or two days longer from the great scarcity of game and the difficult access of the coun-

try, . . . we determined to return in the morning as far as the quaw-mash flatts . . . (Big Disappointment) . . . by returning to the quaw-mash flats we shall sooner be informed whether or not we can pro-cure a guide to conduct us through the mountains; should we fail in procuring one, we have determined to wrisk a passage on the following plan immediately, because should we wait much longer or untill the snow desolves in such manner as to enable us to fol-low the road we cannot hope to reach the United States this win-ter; this is that Capt. C. [Clark] or myself shall take four of our most expert woodsmen with three or four of our best horses and proceed two days in advance taking a plentifull supply of provi-sion. for this party to follow the road by the marks which the bag-gage of the indians has made in many places on the sides of the trees by rubing against them, and to blaize the trees with a toma-hawk as they proceeded, that after proceeding two days in advance of hungary creek two of those men would be sent back to the main party who by the time of their return to Hungary Creek would have reached that place. the men so returning would be enabled to in-form the main party of the probable success of the proceeding party in finding the road and of their probable progress, in order that should it be necessary, the main party by the delay of a day or two at hungary creek, should give the advance time to mark the road through before the main party could overtake them, and thus prevent delay on the part of the rout where no food is to be ob-tained for our horses, should it so happen that the advance could not find the road by the marks on the trees after attempting it for two days, the whole of [them] then would return to the main party. in which case we would bring back our baggage and attempt a pas-sage over these mountains through the country of the Shoshones further to the South by way of the main S. Westerly fork of Lewis's river and Madison or Gallatin's rivers, where from the information of the Chopunnish there is a passage which at this season of the year is not obstructed by snow, though the round is very distant and would require at least a month in it's performance. . . . the only di-ficulty is find the road, and I think the plan we have devised will succeed even should we not be enabled to obtain a guide. Although the snow may be stated on an average at 10 feet deep yet arround the bodies of the trees it has desolved much more than in other parts not being generally more than one or two feet deep immedi-ately at the roots of the trees, and of course the marks left by the rubing of the indian baggage against them is not concealed.

**Argentina Revolts Against Spanish Rule:
May 25, 1810**

The Argentine Revolution Was a Milestone for Freedom

by Ricardo Levene

Argentina's revolution of May 25, 1810, was connected to the European wars and events in Spain, which ruled the colony of Argentina. Napoléon's invasion and takeover of Spain had consequences throughout Latin America, beginning in the Argentinian capital of Buenos Aires. When news of the French conquest of the last Spanish outpost arrived in Buenos Aires, local leaders of that city held a *cabildo abierto* (open town meeting). The Spanish viceroy in charge of the city, Balthasar de Cisneros, was deposed, since the French conquest meant that Spain's administration was no longer in effect. A junta (governing council) was elected at the meeting and declared its authority in the city. Thus the first independent government of the region was established. This action inspired unrest throughout the Latin American colonies for the next decade. Argentina itself declared independence from Spain on July 9, 1916.

In the selection that follows, Ricardo Levene investigates the internal and external causes of the May revolution. He also provides details about the unrest in Argentina and the key figures who participated in the revolution. Levene concludes that the revolution in Argentina was a milestone in the history of free peoples.

Ricardo Levene, "The Revolution," *A History of Argentina*, translated and edited by William Spence Robertson. Chapel Hill: The University of North Carolina Press, 1937. Copyright © 1937 by The University of North Carolina Press. Renewed in 1965 by Gertrude M. Robinson. Reproduced by permission of the publisher.

Historian Ricardo Levene, PhD, had a distinguished career as a scholar and writer. The history of Argentina was Levene's field of expertise.

The revolution was carried out in the name of Ferdinand VII [heir to the kingdom of Spain, whom Napoléon forced into abdication in 1808]. Was this the truth? Historic revolutions are produced as natural phenomena at the precise moment determined by historic and social conditions. They are produced; they come to life; and, in the milieu of reality which surround them, and which is their atmosphere, they live or die. If they triumph, reality and social conditions nourish them; they grow; and they do their work. The Revolution of 1810, born as a popular, democratic, and spontaneous movement, gathered strength; it extended its influence powerfully and triumphed. Because of that, though promoted in the name of the king, it acted against him, because it was stronger and because it was a social revolution. The invocation which the patriots made of the name of the captive king has been appropriately styled the "mask of Ferdinand." It is known that the idea of emancipation had been formulated in organic and explicit terms some years earlier by a nucleus of patriots which gradually enlarged from the time that they embraced the plan of independence under an English protectorate or the coronation of Princess Carlota as monarch of La Plata until they secured the meeting of the cabildo abierto [open town meeting] of May 22.

Internal Causes

The causes of the May Revolution may be classified as internal and external. The internal causes, as the name indicates, are those elaborated and prepared within the colonial society; and the external causes are those influences and events that affected conditions from without and coöperated in the movement of May.

The internal causes include the economic, political, and intellectual antecedents and also the English invasions. By an economic cause is meant the condition of richness and commerce in the colony as a result of the prevailing régime. During the last years of Spanish domination there took place at the same time, on the one hand, active movements of the monopolistic merchants, for the purpose of obtaining concessions and special privileges for their commerce, and, on the other hand, movements of the landowners, laborers, national merchants, and foreigners domiciled in the country who pleaded for the free exportation of its products. The documents of this last category in the seventeenth century are characterized by opposition to the monopolistic economic policy of Peru, and at the end of the eighteenth century, after the promulgation of the regulations concerning free commerce between Spain and the Indies (1778), the struggle is interpreted in Buenos Aires as one of opposing interests against the monopolistic clique. Let one remember the *Representación de los Labradores* (*Memorial of the Farmers*) of 1793 asking for free trade in grains; the representation of the landowners of Buenos Aires and Montevideo in 1794 with regard to the means of promoting the exportation of beef; the debates that took place in the commercial tribunal because of the petition to obtain the revocation of the privilege of commerce with the colonies of other nations than Spain, in which Marcó del Pont, Escalada, Fernández, and others defended national interests; the memorials of Belgrano; the liberal reports of the administrator of the customs, Ángel Izquierdo; and the subsequent representations that were made whenever the conflict started: a struggle of opposing interests which had its most complete expression in the report concerning the free admission of English goods. . . .

On its part after the reconquest, the old group of monopolists, which was represented by a nucleus of Spaniards, with seats in the cabildo and the commercial tribunal and with trade relations, tried to utilize the benefits of the victory for itself and against Platean interests by making use of that prestige before the king. In fact the cabildo had already appointed [Argentine statesman Juan] Pueyrredón its deputy in Spain and, among other instructions, he was directed to solicit an absolute and general prohibition of trade with foreigners. In addition, the monopolistic merchants, assembled in a general junta, selected for the same purpose José Fernández de Castro, who was to make clear to the court the grave evils that resulted to Spanish America from "allowing the colonies freely to engage in foreign commerce, from allowing the slave trade, and from special concessions." The peculiar fact in regard to this last mission is that toward the end of 1809, Fernández de Castro continued to solicit in Spain the revocation of the privileges granted to foreign commerce while in Buenos Aires, by virtue of an act of November 6, 1809, such commerce was actually permitted.

As may be deduced from these data, the question of free commerce or monopolized commerce agitated the merchants of Buenos Aires, and divided them into factions even during the early years of the nineteenth century. . . .

Political Factors

The second internal cause of the May Revolution is political in character. Just as reactions took place in the economic order against the prevailing commercial system by divers facts which we have just mentioned, so, too, various reactions of the people took place against the governmental régime during the colonial era. These reactions occurred in the form of revolutionary explosions, scattered throughout the sixteenth century, but were of a more organic and definite nature during the seventeenth and eighteenth centuries. During the age of the viceroys, we can also distinguish the following stages of reaction against the prevailing political régime: (1) after the English invasions, the people had brought about the reconquest and the defense of Buenos Aires by their own strength, and they then appeared as a powerful entity; (2) in the cabildo abierto of August 14, 1806, and the junta of war of February 10, 1807, the people, declaring themselves to be sovereign, forced [Marques de] Sobremonte to cease ruling and designated [Jacques de] Liniers, the hero of the war with the English, as commander of the troops; (3) on May 25 and July 16, 1809, two important revolutionary movements occurred at Chuquisada and La Paz; and lastly in the cabildo abierto of May 22, 1810, the people ordered that Viceroy Cisneros should cease to rule.

The episode of a political character which should be considered is the Napoleonic invasion of Spain. As a result of this fact, a fundamental political revolution took place in Spain that soon extended to the New World. I refer to the reversion of power to the people when the king was a prisoner, and from the breast of the people the power was constituted in the form of juntas. The supreme junta of Seville succeeded in making itself superior to all the other peninsular juntas and to the authorities of the Indies. When it was dissolved because of the advance of the French armies, the people of Spanish America claimed the right to form juntas as had been done in Spain—such was the pretext for the revolution throughout Spanish America. Upon the fall of the junta of Seville, juntas of government were established at Buenos Aires, Caracas, Mexico, and Santiago de Chile. In the cabildo abierto of May 22 in Buenos Aires, the patriot [Juan] Castelli developed the theory of a crisis in Spanish political law and the doctrine that the *poder magestas* had reverted to the people.

From this viewpoint the Revolution of 1810 should be explained as a stage in the disintegration of the Spanish monarchy. The intellectual antecedents of the movement include the diffusion of liberal ideas . . . and the formation of the revolutionary conscience. The economic, political, and intellectual causes are thus the fundamental causes of the May Revolution that can be explained as the historical resultant of the events and the antecedents which determined its outburst.

The English invasions should also be mentioned among the internal causes of the revolution; for they defined and reënforced the preëxisting sentiment in favor of independence. After 1806 and 1807, event followed event in rapid succession, and the progress of the revolution was accelerated. . . .

External Causes

The external causes of the May Revolution were the North American Revolution and the French Revolution. The first began in 1776. Its immediate cause was the attempt of the English parliament to lay duties upon tea, glass, and stamped paper payable by the North American colonists. These colonists then pleaded a principle of English public law by virtue of which the people should only pay the duties voted by their representatives. The colonists rose in arms, and a few years later as the revolution triumphed, they were emancipated. The North American Revolution had an influence on the May Revolution and on the emancipation of all the Spanish colonies in America for three reasons: (1) because it furnished an example for the Spanish-Americans to imitate; (2) because Spain coöperated in the emancipation of the colonies of North America without considering that it was the mistress of other colonies that might follow the example of the Thirteen Colonies; (3) as a consequence of the aid that Spain furnished to the North American colonies, England waged war upon Spain (1779–1783), an event which produced grave economic disturbances in Spanish America. As a result of such events, England intensified its campaign, with the idea of promoting the emancipation of the Spanish colonies.

In fact, there had occurred in Spanish America many events which presaged the approaching movement of emancipation. Some historians believe that the minister of the king of Spain,

Count Aranda, had proposed to his sovereign that in order to dominate that movement and to prevent the absolute loss of the colonies—so extensive and so distant from the motherland—it would be convenient to found three monarchies (in Mexico, Peru, and La Plata) headed by princes of the reigning Spanish dynasty. But King Charles III did not attach great importance to these events, and soon afterward the revolution broke out which Count Aranda had foreseen and tried to avoid.

Another external cause of the May Revolution is the French Revolution of 1789. The influence of this revolution was universal, for it formulated "The Declaration of the Rights of Man," which included liberty, equality, property, and the sovereignty of the people. The ideas of the French Revolution spread throughout the world, through its writers and philosophers. To the distant colony of La Plata those ideas of liberty and sovereignty also came. Thus, in the University of Chuquisaca the patriots studied the jurists and historians of the Indies and the French philosophers: Moreno republished a translation of Rousseau's *Social Contract.*

A Milestone

The Argentine Revolution of 1810 is a milestone in the history of free peoples. Like the French Revolution and the Revolution in North America, the May Revolution was a revolution of principles; it overthrew one régime to supplant it by another, which proved to be liberal in its laws and guarantees. It began in Buenos Aires on May 25, 1810, and spread throughout the entire vice-royalty; on July 9, 1816, it became general for all the United Provinces of La Plata; and, in 1817, the cause of the revolution was Americanized, for it was extended to Chile, Peru, and Ecuador. The May Revolution, born in Buenos Aires in 1810, was accordingly continental and American in its ends and great consequences. We may affirm that this revolution had its "declaration of rights"; for it proclaimed and made effective the rights of political, intellectual, and commercial liberty and guaranteed the principles of equality among all men and justice founded upon law.

The Legacy of America's Most Obscure War

by Donald R. Hickey

After years of attempting to stay neutral, the United States finally became entangled in the Napoleonic Wars in the beginning of the nineteenth century. The ongoing struggle between Great Britain and France put significant economic pressure on the United States. Because the American Revolution was a recent memory, the tension that historically existed between Great Britain and the United States needed little to escalate to a full-fledged war.

U.S. president James Madison cited impressments (maritime procurements by force of American seamen), violations of neutrality, and incitement of Native Americans on the western frontier as some of the recent affronts from Great Britain. He and some other leaders advocated war in an effort to quell perceived British attempts at subordinating the United States. The war, against which there was sharp opposition due to unclear objectives, began on June 18, 1812, and ended on February 17, 1815. The War of 1812 has often been considered indecisive because the war aims were not addressed during the peace settlement (the Treaty of Ghent) and were not relevant matters by the war's end.

Donald R. Hickey, in the following excerpt, assesses the importance of the war as well as its consequences and legacies. He also considers some of the key leaders and politicians who played a role in the war. Hickey examines the impact of the war on both domestic and international affairs.

Donald R. Hickey, *The War of 1812: A Short History*. Chicago: University of Illinois Press, 1995. Copyright © 1995 by the Board of Trustees of the University of Illinois. Reproduced by permission.

Professor of history Donald R. Hickey of Wayne State College has published widely on the subject of early American history. He has won several awards for his publications.

The War of 1812 is probably our most obscure war. Although a great deal has been written about the conflict, the average American is only vaguely aware of why we fought or who the enemy was. Even those who know something about the contest are likely to remember only a few dramatic moments, such as the Battle of New Orleans, the burning of the nation's capital, or the writing of "The Star-Spangled Banner."

Why is this war so obscure? One reason is that no great president is associated with the conflict. Although his enemies called it "Mr. Madison's War," James Madison hardly measures up to such war leaders as Abraham Lincoln, Woodrow Wilson, or Franklin Roosevelt. In addition, the great generals in this war—Andrew Jackson and Winfield Scott—were unable to turn the tide because each was confined to a secondary theater of operations. No one like George Washington, Ulysses Grant, or Dwight Eisenhower emerged to put his stamp on the war and carry the nation to victory.

An Obscure War

Another reason for the obscurity of this war is that (like many wars) its causes are complex and still subject to debate. Some scholars have argued for the primacy of maritime causes, claiming that the United States went to war to force the British to give up the Orders in Council and impressment. In contemporary parlance, the war was fought for "free trade and sailors' rights." Other writers have emphasized western aims—the desire to conquer Canada to secure additional farmland or to put an end to British influence over American Indians. Still others have focused on political causes, asserting that the Republicans embraced war as a means of forging party unity, maintaining power, and silencing the Federalists. Yet another group has stressed ideological factors— the desire to uphold the prestige of the Republic, preserve national honor, and ensure the continued vitality of republican institutions. The decision for war, in other words, has been attributed to a wide variety of motives.

If the causes of the war are unclear, so too are the consequences. The United States has won most of its wars, often emerging with significant concessions from the enemy, but the War of 1812 was different. Far from bringing the enemy to terms, the nation was lucky to escape without making extensive concessions itself. The Treaty of Ghent (which ended the conflict) said nothing about the issues that had caused the war and contained nothing to suggest that the United States had achieved its aims. Instead, it merely provided for returning to the *status quo ante bellum*—the state of affairs existing before the war.

The prosecution of the war was marred by considerable bungling and mismanagement. This was partly due to the nature of the Republic. The nation was too young and immature—and its government too feeble and inexperienced—to prosecute a major war efficiently. Politics also played a part. Federalists vigorously opposed the conflict, and so did some Republicans. Even those who supported the war feuded among themselves and never displayed the sort of patriotic enthusiasm that has been so evident in most other wars the United States has fought. The advocates of war appeared to support the conflict with their heads more than with their hearts, and with their hearts more than with their purses. As a result, efforts to recruit men and raise money lagged consistently behind need.

Characteristics and Significance

Despite the bungling and half-hearted support that characterized this conflict, the War of 1812 was not without its stirring moments and splendid victories. The crushing defeat of the British at New Orleans, the rousing defense of Baltimore, and the naval triumphs on the northern lakes and the high seas all showed that with proper leadership and training American fighting men could hold their own against the well-drilled and battle-hardened regulars of Great Britain.

The war also produced its share of heroes—people whose reputations were enhanced by military or government service. The war helped catapult four men into the presidency—Andrew Jackson, John Quincy Adams, James Monroe, and William Henry Harrison—and three men into the vice presidency—Daniel D. Tompkins, John C. Calhoun, and Richard M. Johnson. The war also gave a significant boost to the political or military careers of other men, most notably Henry Clay, Jacob Brown, and Winfield Scott. Indeed, for many ambitious young men, the war offered an excellent launching pad for a career.

In some ways the War of 1812 looked to the past more than to the future. As the second and last war the United States fought against Great Britain, it echoed the ideology and issues of the American Revolution. It was the second and last time that the United States was the underdog in a war and the second and last time that the nation tried to conquer Canada. The war was unique in generating such vigorous political opposition and nearly unique in ending in a draw. Although most Americans pretended they had won the war—even calling it a "second war of independence"—they could point to few concrete gains to support this claim.

It is this lack of success that may best explain why the war is so little remembered. Americans have characteristically judged their wars on the basis of their success. The best-known wars—the Revolution, the Civil War, and World War II—were all spectacular successes. Although many people remembered the War of 1812 as a success, it was actually a failure, and perhaps this is why it attracts so little attention today.

The obscurity of this war, however, should not blind us to its significance, for it was an important turning point, a great watershed, in the history of the young Republic. It concluded almost a quarter of a century of troubled diplomacy and partisan politics and ushered in the Era of Good Feelings. It marked the end of the Federalist party but the vindication of Federalist policies, many of which were adopted by Republicans during or after the war. It also broke the power of American Indians and reinforced the powerful undercurrent of Anglophobia that had been present in American society since the Revolution. Above all, it promoted national self-confidence and encouraged the heady expansionism that lay at the heart of American foreign policy for the rest of the century. Although looking to the past, the war was fraught with consequences for the future, and for this reason it is worth studying today. . . .

State of Affairs with England

The War of 1812 is often called America's "second war of independence." The issues and ideology of this conflict did echo those of the Revolution, but the supposed threat to American independence in 1812 was more imagined than real. It existed mainly in the minds of thin-skinned Republicans who were unable to shed the ideological legacy of the Revolution and interpreted all British actions accordingly.

There is no denying that British encroachments on American rights were both real and serious. Throughout this period, however, the focus of British policy was always on Europe. The overriding objective of the British government was to secure the defeat of France, and all else was subordinated to this purpose. Britain's aim, in other words, was not to subvert American independence but to win the war in Europe. Once this objective was achieved, its infringements on American rights would cease.

Not only did Republicans misread British intentions, but throughout this turbulent era they consistently overrated America's ability to win concessions. "We have considered ourselves of too much importance in the scale of nations," Daniel Sheffey, a Virginia Federalist, said. "It has led us into great errors. Instead of yielding to circumstances, which human power cannot control, we have imagined that our own destiny, and that of other nations, was in our hands, to be regulated as we thought proper." Sheffey's analysis was borne out, not only by the restrictive system but also by the war.

The War of 1812 lasted only two years and eight months—from June 18, 1812, to February 17, 1815. Though the war was not long, the United States was beset by problems from the beginning. Many of the nation's military leaders were incompetent, and enlistments in the army and navy lagged behind need. The militia was costly and inefficient and repeatedly refused to cross into Canada or to hold its position under enemy fire. In addition, the government found it difficult to borrow money, and the nation's finances became increasingly chaotic. There was also extensive trade with the enemy, trade in which Federalists and Republicans alike freely took part. A combination of Federalist opposition, Republican factionalism, and general public apathy undermined the entire war effort.

Congress was partly responsible for this state of affairs. Endless debate and deep divisions delayed or prevented the adoption of much-needed legislation. Congress was particularly negligent on financial matters. Hoping for a quick war and fearing the political consequences of unpopular measures, Republicans postponed internal taxes and delayed a national bank. As a result, public credit collapsed in 1814, and a general suspension of specie payments ensued. If the contest had continued much longer, the Revolutionary War phrase "not worth a continental" might have been replaced by "not worth a treasury note."

President Madison's Role

A strong president might have overcome some of these problems, but Madison was one of the weakest war leaders in the nation's history. Although his opponents called the contest "Mr. Madison's War," it never bore his stamp. Cautious, shy, and circumspect, Madison was unable to supply the bold and vigorous leadership that was needed. "Mr. Madison is wholly unfit for the storms of war," Henry Clay observed. "Nature has cast him in too benevolent a mould."

In some respects, to be sure, Madison's caution served the nation well. Unlike other war presidents, he showed remarkable respect for the civil rights of his domestic foes. Despite pleas from other Republicans, he refused to resort to a sedition law. Even though Federalists had to face mob violence (particularly at the beginning of the war), they never had to contend with government repression. Madison's treatment of prisoners of war was also commendably humane, and his circumspect policy on disaffection in New England was undoubtedly well judged too.

In other ways, however, Madison's cautious brand of leadership undermined the nation's war effort. He allowed such incompetents as William Eustis and Paul Hamilton to hold key positions, and he tolerated intrigues and backbiting among his closest advisers. Madison was also slow to get rid of incompetent generals in the field and to promote officers who had proven themselves in battle. Because he lacked a commanding influence in Congress, he was unable to secure vital legislation, and because he lacked a strong following in the country, he was unable to inspire people to open their hearts and purses.

No doubt poor leadership in Washington and in the field drove up the cost of this war. The battle casualties were comparatively light: 2,260 killed and 4,505 wounded. The number of nonbattle deaths—mostly from disease—was probably about 17,000. The army executed an additional 205 men, mainly for repeated desertion, and the navy executed a few men too. Some men who had served on privateers also died in the war, primarily from disease in British prisons. There were a few civilian casualties as well—mostly victims of Indian raids in the West. In all, the number of American deaths attributable to the war was probably about 20,000.

The financial cost of the war (excluding property damage, lost economic opportunities, and land bounties) was $158 million. This includes $93 million in army and navy expenditures, $16 million for interest on the war loans, and $49 million in veterans' benefits. (The last veteran died in 1905, the last pensioner—the daughter of a veteran—in 1946.) The national debt, which Republicans had reduced from $83 million in 1801 to $45 million in 1812, soared to $127 million by the end of 1815.

Consequences of the War

What did the war accomplish? Although militarily the conflict ended in a draw, in a larger sense it represented a failure for Republican policymakers. The nation was unable to conquer Canada or to achieve any of its maritime goals. Indeed, these issues were not even mentioned in the peace treaty, which merely provided for restoring all conquered territory and returning to the *status quo ante bellum.*

In other ways, however, the war was fraught with consequences. The United States annexed part of Spanish West Florida in 1813—the only permanent land acquisition made during the war, though it came at the expense of a neutral power rather than the enemy.

The war also broke the power of the Indians in the Old West. The attempts of Tecumseh and the Prophet in the Northwest and of the Red Sticks in the Southwest to halt the tide of American expansion ended in failure. Instead, the Indian wars gave the United States government both the excuse and the incentive to accelerate the forced removal of the eastern tribes to lands beyond the Mississippi River. Never again would Indians seriously threaten the United States, and never again would a foreign nation tamper with American Indians. The subjugation of the Indians, in turn, promoted manifest destiny and the westward movement. The heady nationalism and expansionism that characterized American foreign policy throughout the nineteenth century was at least partly a result of the War of 1812.

Even though the war stimulated nationalism, it was also an important benchmark in the history of American sectionalism. To retain control of their militia and obstruct war measures, New England Federalists resurrected the states' rights doctrine that Virginia Republicans had used in the late 1790s to fight the alien and sedition laws. This same doctrine would later flourish in the South, until a northern victory in the Civil War delivered a body blow to the whole notion of states' rights.

The war also stimulated peacetime defense spending. In his message to Congress announcing the end of hostilities, President Madison echoed an old Federalist plea by calling for preparedness. "Experience has taught us," he said, "that a certain degree of preparation for war is not only indispensable to avert disasters in the onset, but affords also the best security for the continuance of peace." Congress agreed. The peacetime army was fixed at 10,000 men in 1815 (three times what it had been in 1802), and the construction of nine ships-of-the-line and twelve heavy frigates was authorized in 1816. Congress also launched a far-reaching program to fortify the coast, appropriating almost $8.5 million for this purpose between 1816 and 1829.

The war affected the American military establishment in another way. Those officers who had outlived their usefulness—Alexander Smyth, James Wilkinson, Wade Hampton, and the like—were cast aside during the war to make room for younger men, such as Jacob Brown, Winfield Scott, Edmund Gaines, Alexander Macomb, and Andrew Jackson. As a result, the American army had a decidedly new look by 1815. Some navy officers also burned their names into the history books. Among these were Oliver Perry, Thomas Macdonough, Isaac Hull, William Bainbridge, Stephen Decatur, and Charles Stewart.

The war had a dramatic impact on the American economy too. Unlike most American wars, this one did not generate a general economic boom. According to Thomas Jefferson, whose heavy debts became unmanageable during the war, the conflict "arrested the course of the most remarkable tide of prosperity any nation ever experienced." Although people in the middle and western states prospered, those in New England and the South did not. Manufacturing thrived because of the absence of British competition, but whatever gains were made in this sector of the economy were dwarfed by heavy losses in fishing and commerce. For most Americans, the economic opportunities were greater before and after the war than during it.

Legacies of the War

The war left an enduring legacy of Anglophobia in the United States. Hatred of England, originally kindled by the American Revolution, was further inflamed by the War of 1812—particularly by the Indian atrocities in the West and British depredations in the Chesapeake.

Britain's treatment of American prisoners of war further intensified this Anglophobia. At one time or another about 20,000 Americans, mostly men who had served on privateers, were held in British prisons. British officials often treated these prisoners roughly. Even before the war was over, stories of abuse began to filter back to the United States. After the war ended, the trickle of stories became a torrent. "The return of our people from British prisons," said *Niles' Register*, "have filled the newspapers with tales of horror."

Some of the stories came from Halifax, where most Americans captured on the northern frontier were held. "All the prisoners that we have yet seen," said the Boston *Patriot*, "agree that their treatment in the Halifax prisons was brutal and barbarous in the extreme."

Other stories came from Dartmoor, a damp and dreary prison in southwestern England. By the end of the war, "this accursed place," as one prisoner called it, housed some 5,000 Americans. Trouble at Dartmoor reached a climax on April 6, 1815—almost two months after the war ended—when a dispute over responsibility for transporting the men home delayed repatriation. Anxious to regain their freedom, the prisoners became unruly, and British soldiers fired on them, killing six and wounding sixty others.

Americans did not soon forget the brutality of the war. As early as 1813, the House of Representatives published a study—with extensive documentation—that criticized Great Britain for the Indian atrocities, the Chesapeake depredations, and the mistreatment of prisoners. Other stories kept the embers of hatred alive for decades. Long after the conflict was over, *Niles' Register* published war-related anecdotes and documents that showed the British in a bad light, and some nineteenth-century histories continued this tradition by focusing on Britain's misdeeds.

Another legacy of the war was the enhanced reputation that the United States enjoyed in Europe. Although America's performance in the war was mixed, it earned the respect of Europe. "The Americans," said Augustus J. Foster, "have had the satisfaction of proving their courage—they have brought us to speak of them with respect."

The British were careful not to impress any Americans when the Royal Navy went back on a war footing during Napoleon's Hundred Days in 1815. In fact, Americans were never again subjected to those dubious maritime practices that had caused the war. With Europe generally at peace in the century after Waterloo, the Great Powers had no interest in regulating America's trade or tampering with its merchant marine. The United States had ample time to grow and to husband its strength so that it could meet the Great Powers on an equal footing in the next great conflict—World War I.

9 The Brothers Grimm Publish a Fairy-Tale Collection: 1812

Grimms' Collection Explores Universal Themes

by Bruno Bettelheim

In 1812 brothers Jakob and Wilhelm Grimm published their first collection of fairy tales, *Kinder-und Hausmärchen* (*Tales of Children and the Home*). As German scholars, they viewed themselves as folklorists preserving the oral traditions of Germany. Both the cultural movement of romanticism and the Napoleonic Wars inspired in the Brothers Grimm a nationalist penchant for looking into the past.

The fairy tales, including the well-known stories of Hansel and Gretel, Cinderella, and Snow White, were collected by recording stories narrated by German peasants and villagers. The brothers then rewrote and edited the stories based on the oral tales. These fairy tales, which remain popular to the present day, influenced generations of folklorists and children's story writers.

In the following selection, Bruno Bettelheim illustrates the role of Grimms' fairy tales in the history of folklore collection and German cultural history. He describes the motivations of the Brothers Grimm as well as their legacy. Bettelheim, using the story of Hansel and Gretel as an example, also notes that one can learn from the moral symbolism of the tales.

Bruno Bettelheim, "Foreword," *Jakob and Wilhelm Grimm and Others: German Fairy Tales*, edited by Helmut Brackert and Volkmar Sander. New York: Continuum, 1985. Copyright © 1985 by the Continuum Publishing Company. Foreword Copyright © 1985 by Bruno Bettelheim. All rights reserved. Reproduced by permission.

Bruno Bettelheim was a well-known developmental psychologist whose influential writings focused on child development.

A ll fairy tales are folktales, but not all folktales are fairy tales, since in most folktales neither fairies nor wizards appear. Folktales are part of the most ancient literature. They were told and retold everywhere, since the beginning of time, all over the world. Only during the Enlightenment were these tales shunned in educated circles, although even there they continued to be enjoyed by children and ordinary people. All this changed practically overnight when the brothers Grimm published their *Kinder und Hausmärchen (Children's and Household Tales)* in 1812. The success of their collection was so great and immediate that ever since then the folktales of all nations have been and still are collected, studied, and, most important, appreciated for their poetic merit. Without their pioneering effort, for example, [folklorist Ludwig] Bechstein . . . would not have embarked on his collection of folktales.

The brothers Grimm, however, were not the first to collect and publish folktales. As early as 1637, Gianbattista Basile's *Pentamerone* appeared which contained, for example, a Neapolitan version of Snow White. His collection remained virtually unknown until modern times because very few people understood the Neapolitan dialect in which the tales Basile collected were told. At the end of the seventeenth century Charles Perrault published a number of French tales, and so did Mme. d'Aulnoy in her *Contes nouvelles ou les fées à la mode.* Both authors, while basing their stories on then well-known French tales, did indeed rework them *à la mode.* They moralized and prettified them and in doing so did tort to their true spirit. At the beginning of the eighteenth century Abbé Antoine Galland translated *Thousand and One Nights* into French, but in such orientalizing fashion that they found attention only as strange curiosities which fitted well into the period's fascination with chinoiseries.

This early interest in collecting and publishing folktales evaporated during the following period of the Enlightenment, when it was thought that such fantastic tales did not merit the attention of educated persons, that the irrational and supernatural features of which many of these tales abound are offensive to the intelligent person who was supposed to be interested only in what was rational. When any attention was paid to these tales, it was only after they had been changed beyond recognition, after their original themes had been trivialized and adapted to what was the current style of polite literature. Even [Johann] Musäus, who published the *Volksmärchen der Deutschen* [*German Folktales*] in five volumes from 1782 to 1787 retold them to conform to the literary taste of the educated classes of his day. None of these early collectors of folktales considered them worthy of publication in the form in which they were told; they all felt the need to edit them in polite language and as if they contained only lofty ideas.

Motivations of the Brothers Grimm

The attitude with which Jakob Grimm, born in 1785, and his brother Wilhelm, born a year later, approached the task of collecting and publishing fairy tales was an entirely different one. The Napoleonic wars had aroused their nationalistic feelings, while the Romantic movement had stimulated their interest in the German past. While their *Kinder und Hausmärchen* established their worldwide reputation which since then has increased from year to year, and while they created German folklore as a discipline, it was possibly their *German Dictionary* that was their *magnum opus*. It represents a new departure in lexicography, incomparable in its day. Without the Grimms' efforts in pioneering modern lexicography, the *Oxford English Dictionary* might never have come into being, or in a quite different form, since it was their *German Dictionary* which broke entirely new scholarly ground.

It was their respect for the German past which induced them to try to retell these ancient tales the way they had been told and retold in the past. In their introduction to the first volume of these tales, published in 1812, they stated their intentions: "We have taken pains to record these tales as untouched as was possible. . . . No situation has been added, or prettified, or altered, for we hesitated to expand tales that were already so rich in their own analogies and reminiscences. . . . There is no other collection in this manner existent in Germany, for people have almost always used the tales only as narrative material in order to make larger stories out of them which, arbitrarily expanded and changed, may still have some value but took from children what was properly theirs and gave them nothing in return. Even those who took thought in the matter could not help mixing in mannerisms which were supplied by the poetic mode of the time; almost always there has been a lack of diligence in collecting."

It is not that the brothers did not take some liberties with the tales when they published them. They often tightened the plot or clarified it to obtain a more closely knit tale. It was their genius that out of several versions of the same tale they wove one which in the end was truer to the spirit of the folktale, as later research taught us to recognize, than was the particular way in which their informers, such as "Old Marie," the housekeeper of their neighbors, the Wild family, or Gretchen Wild, one of the daughters, told them. Thanks to the brothers' poetic and historic genius they recognized what in the versions they were told was the product of the imagination of the person who told the story and what was the essential tale that lay behind it, and this they created or rather re-created by the small changes they introduced into the tale they had been told.

The German poet Ludwig Uhland said that the brothers Grimm "had spun a golden thread of poetry which, thanks to them, runs through all of German life." The brothers succeeded in lifting a veil which up to their time had obscured most of the German folk literature of the past. Not only that, due to the enormous success of their collection, fairy tales captured the imagination of all of Europe, and eventually of all continents, and brought about a recognition of the importance of the fairy tales of all people.

Learning from the Tales

When Achim von Arnim, another German Romantic poet, objected to Jakob Grimm that not all tales were truly children's stories, he replied that it was wrong to distinguish between the interests of adults and children, stressing that all ages can enjoy these tales, that they have much to offer to anyone who opens himself to their beauty, that they have meaning to young and old alike, although on different levels of appreciation.

On various occasions both brothers emphasized that children could learn a great deal from these stories. Jakob Grimm, in his dedication of their book to a friend, wrote that he hoped that his child would learn a great deal from it, because "it is our firm intention that the book be regarded as an educational book." And Wilhelm wrote to their friend and mentor Friedrich Karl von Savigny, in whose library they had first become acquainted with German literary antiquities, "We really wished the tales to be an educational book, since I know nothing that is more nourishing, more innocent and refreshing for childlike powers and nature."

When the brothers Grimm spoke of the education children can

derive from these tales, they had not school learning in mind, but education in the best, the highest humanistic sense, an education that,
as it nourishes the child's mind, teaches him much about his very
nature, aspects of which he can understand only when these are presented to him in the symbolic language of art which speaks directly
to his deepest longings, relieves his anxieties, kindles his hopes so
that he can meet the vagaries of life with greater confidence.

Every person can discover only in his own way what appeals to
him of the literary, the poetic qualities of these stories, and he can
do so only by listening to or reading the stories, letting sink in
what they tell about the child in all of us. For this reason I shall
try in the following remarks to illustrate, by means of one well-
known story, what some of the "educational" merits of these stories are, how they indeed help the child to become more deeply
aware of his very nature.

The poet Rainer Maria Rilke, at the beginning of the first of the
Duino Elegies, reveals what forms the essence of great art:
"Beauty is nothing but the beginning of terror we are still just able
to bear, and why we adore it so is because it serenely disdains to
destroy us." This certainly is true for most fairy tales. Their beauty
is inextricably interwoven with the terror they arouse and the
hero's—and with it our—rescue at the happy ending. Fairy tales
present to us this essence of beauty in a most concise manner, and
in ways in which it can be comprehended even by the most naive
peruser of this literature, even by the young child.

Beginning in a setting akin to our most ordinary existence, fairy
tales take us in a short and dramatic move to the very edge of the
abyss, as does any true exploration of the meaning of life, of its
deeper purpose, as does any serious effort to know ourselves that
penetrates beyond the surface of our being and reaches into the
darker recesses of our mind, particularly those which we desire not
to recognize. These are the aspects of our existence which threaten
us most, which are likely to cause our troubles, but which also en-
dow our existence with some of its deepest meaning. This darkness
within ourselves is what we need most to become acquainted with
if we want to know ourselves. The fairy tale, after having made us
tremble by taking us to the edge of the abyss, after having forced
us to face evil and all the darkness within man, after having acquainted us with what we rather wish to avoid, serenely rescues us.
In the course of the story, as we identify with its hero, we gain the
ability to live a richer and more meaningful life on a much higher

plane than the one on which we found ourselves at the story's beginning, where the hero, who is our mirror image, was forced to
embark on his perilous voyage of self-discovery.

Hänsel and Gretel

Hänsel and Gretel are two very ordinary children when we meet
them at the beginning of their story. Like most children, they are
assailed in the darkness of the night by anxious fantasies about
their parents' plans to get rid of them, are beset by starvation anxiety. Convinced that they cannot take care of themselves, they
know only one way to be safe: to hang on most determinedly to
what they are most familiar with: their home, their mother's apron
strings. But it will no longer do. Like all children, Hänsel and Gretel must learn not only to become able to fend for themselves but
also to meet the dark aspects of life. Most of all they must learn
to combat their primitive anxieties about being starved and devoured, which are closely connected with their deep oral cravings
tempting them to eat even what seems to offer most pleasant shel-
ter, symbolized by the gingerbread house. They will not be able
to be themselves nor to meet the world successfully unless they
have first courageously faced their anxious fantasy of the archetypical bad, devouring mother. It is an image which every child
creates out of his experience of wishing to eat up his mother so
that she will never be able to desert him even for a moment, and
of his fear that, in retaliation, the mother will eat him up. It is an
image as old as the child's nursing experience when, as he sucks
from the breast—or from the bottle which he experiences as a
poor substitute for the breast—he imagines himself as incorpo-
rating the mother. It is the fear of the bad mother which is the inescapable reverse image of the all-loving mother, the counterpart
of the giving and protective mother whose image is replaced when
she makes demands, criticizes, and even occasionally punishes the
infant. It is the consequence of the infant's utter dependence on an
all-powerful person, whose intentions the infant cannot fathom
and which therefore may be evil. All of this is symbolically expressed in the fairy tale by the replacement of the all-good mother,
who gave birth to her infant but soon disappears, by the demand-
ing and frustrating stepmother, as in Cinderella and Snow White.
  Hänsel and Gretel encounter their own fantasies about the devouring mother in the form of the witch. This witch hides within
or behind the alluring, wish-fulfilling oral fantasy of the ginger-

bread house, which has its origin in the earliest phase of the child's development when he experiences everything in terms of his orality. At the beginning of the story, we met the archetypical image of the bad mother in its more ordinary form of the depriving and rejecting stepmother, who is intent on forcing the children to learn to shift for themselves, to stop being a burden to their parents, to begin to become masters of their fate. As reluctant as the children are to become their own masters, the fairy tale tells that they will perish unless they do so. Harsh events force them to learn to defeat evil incarnate: the witch. In destroying her they free themselves at the same time from dependence on their orality, and learn to recognize and activate the forces within them of self-protection. This they do as they overcome their fear of the all-destructive figure of the witch, outwit her, and in the end overcome her.

Because Hänsel and Gretel were able to gain control over their nightmarish terror—given tangible form in the figure of the witch—they gained confidence in their own strength to defeat evil and to rescue themselves. Because they succeeded in their battle against the primordial oral anxiety about being devoured, their lives are as if miraculously enriched. This is symbolically expressed in their gaining the witches' jewels which henceforth provide them with a secure livelihood. Having found their own strength and gained the ability to exercise it, they no longer need to live in fear, nor to depend on others for their well being. Life will be good for them forever after.

It was their experience in the dark and pathless forest, it was their encounter with terror, that did all this for them. Finding oneself in a dark impenetrable forest is an ancient literary image for man in need of self-knowledge. Dante evoked it at the beginning of the *Divine Comedy*, but long before him it served as [an] image of man in search [of] himself, of man caught in a moral crisis, of man having to negotiate a developmental impasse, as he wishes to move from a lower to a higher level of self-consciousness. It is the ambience in which Hänsel and Gretel meet the witch. It is the ambience into which the knight errant rides, seeking the greatest adventure man can encounter: to meet and find himself, as he does battle against the forces of evil. This evil, this darkness that surrounds him in the forest, is but a projection of the darkness that resides in himself, and so is the dragon against which he does battle. The dragon is a figment of his imagination onto which he projects all that he cannot accept in himself. By defeating the dragon he wins a moral victory over himself, symbolized by his rescuing the dragon's victim. His victory is gaining permanent access to his higher self which up to then had been held captive, inoperative, by the powers of darkness. Because of their encounter with the witch, Hänsel and Gretel's childish naïvete and utter dependence on others is replaced by a proud maturity which permits them not only to rescue themselves but also their father, who had despaired of his ability to take care of his children. The children, who at the story's beginning had felt themselves the helpless pawns of their parents and of fate, are at its end masters of their destiny and able to take care of their parent. What happier ending to a story can there be?

Symbolism in Fairy Tales

Comprehending what a fairy tale reveals in symbolic form about how one must organize one's life to master its invariable difficulties requires not only repeated listening but also the chance to ponder the tale's meaning to one's heart's delight. Only then can the child begin to understand that the story tries to tell him that he cannot remain forever dependent, cannot expect to be taken care of by others all his life. Only then does the child comprehend the shortcomings of relying for his security on his parents, recognize the advantages of becoming a person in his own right. Only then does he gain the hope that however nightmarishly difficult it may seem to him to dare to become truly himself, it is a task that he can master and be much the better for it. It is a lesson that many fairy tales teach, each in its own and different form, by means of different images and in an esthetic rendering suitable to its content.

Typically, in Hänsel and Gretel as in many other fairy tales, the child protagonists have to meet fearful dangers and to engage in actions requiring great valor before they can gain their just rewards. However the story's hero may have been threatened as the story unfolds, in the end he is rescued. The eventual rescue, complete restoration, and elevation of the hero to a superior existence is characteristic of fairy tales because as works of art their purpose is to acquaint us with the fact not only that life is difficult and often entails dangerous struggles but also that only through the mastery of succeeding crises in our existence can we eventually find our true self. Having achieved this, we then no longer need to live in fear of our childish anxieties.

One might even say that the stories tell the child that he will succeed only because hardships force him to develop his ingenuity, initiative, and independence. There are no fairy tales telling of a child growing into a self-reliant, successful person whose original mother continued to take marvelous care of him all through his growing-up years. Painful as is the process of separation and individuation, fairy tales assure the child that it is a necessary and inescapable developmental task, and one that turns out to be for the best. Cinderella's stepsisters, who are indulged all their lives by their mother who demands nothing of them, come to a very bad end because they never learned to cope with frustration.

Since it has been objected that fairy tales, with their monsters, giants, and witches, scare children unnecessarily, in ending I might mention that every child, all on his own, invents scary figures such as the bogeyman. But also all on his own he feels helpless to cope with them and the anxieties they create in him. The fairy tale shows him that it is not just he who is terrified by such figures but that these stand for universal anxieties, and while on his own the child fears he can never get the better of these terrifying figures of his imagination, fairy tales assure him that the good are always helped and rewarded, and in the end victorious, as even little Gretel can push the evil witch into the oven where she meets her well-deserved fate.

The Brothers Grimm Publish a Fairy-Tale Collection: 1812

Hansel and Gretel

by Jakob and Wilhelm Grimm

The 1812 collection of fairy tales published in Germany by Jakob and Wilhelm Grimm was the first of seven editions of *Kinder-und Haus-märchen (Tales of Children and the Home)* to be released. Since that time, *Grimm's Fairy Tales*, which is the English-version title of the collection, has been translated into over 160 languages. The United States alone has printed more than 120 editions of the work.

Grimm's Fairy Tales contains approximately 210 stories. One of the most well-known tales, "Hansel and Gretel" (alternately spelled "Grethel"), is presented here. In this fairy tale, a brother and sister are sent to the forest by their uncaring stepmother. The children encounter a house made of bread and an ill-intentioned witch, but they eventually escape and make their way back home. Not only can the story be read for its entertainment value but, as with all of Grimm's fairy tales, there are morals to be gleaned. Also, note the treatment of the villain, the harshness of which (in this story and other tales with villains) was often criticized by nineteenth-century readers and educators.

O nce upon a time there dwelt near a large wood a poor woodcutter, with his wife and two children by his former marriage, a little boy called Hansel, and a girl named Grethel. He had little enough to break or bite; and once, when there was a great famine in the land, he could not procure even his daily bread; and as he lay thinking in his bed one evening, rolling about for trouble, he sighed, and said to his wife, "What will become of us? How can we feed our children, when we have no more than we can eat ourselves?"

Jakob and Wilhelm Grimm, "Hansel and Gretel," *Household Stories Collected by the Brothers Grimm*. London: Routledge, 1901.

Into the Forest

"Know, then, my husband," answered she, "we will lead them away, quite early in the morning, into the thickest part of the wood, and there make them a fire, and give them each a little piece of bread; then we will go to our work, and leave them alone, so they will not find the way home again, and we shall be freed from them." "No, wife," replied he, "that I can never do; how can you bring your heart to leave my children all alone in the wood; for the wild beasts will soon come and tear them to pieces?"

"Oh, you simpleton!" said she, "then we must all four die of hunger; you had better plane the coffins for us." But she left him no peace till he consented, saying, "Ah, but I shall regret the poor children."

The two children, however, had not gone to sleep for very hunger, and so they overheard what the stepmother said to their father. Grethel wept bitterly, and said to Hansel, "What will become of us?" "Be quiet, Grethel," said he; "do not cry—I will soon help you." And as soon as their parents had fallen asleep, he got up, put on his coat, and unbarring the back door, slipped out. The moon shone brightly, and the white pebbles which lay before the door seemed like silver pieces, they glittered so brightly. Hansel stooped down, and put as many into his pocket as it would hold; and then going back, he said to Grethel, "Be comforted, dear sister, and sleep in peace; God will not forsake us." And so saying, he went to bed again.

The next morning, before the sun arose, the wife went and awoke the two children. "Get up, you lazy things; we are going into the forest to chop wood." Then she gave them each a piece of bread, saying, "There is something for your dinner; do not eat it before the time, for you will get nothing else." Grethel took the bread in her apron, for Hansel's pocket was full of pebbles; and so they all set out upon their way. When they had gone a little distance, Hansel stood still, and peeped back at the house; and this he repeated several times, till his father said, "Hansel, what are you peeping at, and why do you lag behind? Take care, and remember your legs."

"Ah, father," said Hansel, "I am looking at my white cat sitting upon the roof of the house, and trying to say good-bye." "You simpleton!" said the wife, "that is not a cat; it is only the sun shining on the white chimney." But in reality Hansel was not looking at a cat; but every time he stopped, he dropped a pebble out of his pocket upon the path.

When they came to the middle of the wood, the father told the children to collect wood, and he would make them a fire, so that they should not be cold. So Hansel and Grethel gathered together quite a little mountain of twigs. Then they set fire to them; and as the flame burnt up high, the wife said, "Now, you children, lie down near the fire, and rest yourselves, whilst we go into the forest and chop wood; when we are ready, I will come and call you."

Finding the Way Home

Hansel and Grethel sat down by the fire, and when it was noon, each ate the piece of bread; and because they could hear the blows of an axe, they thought their father was near: but it was not an axe, but a branch which he had bound to a withered tree, so as to be blown to and fro by the wind. They waited so long, that at last their eyes closed from weariness, and they fell fast asleep. When they awoke, it was quite dark, and Grethel began to cry, "How shall we get out of the wood?" But Hansel tried to comfort her by saying, "Wait a little while till the moon rises, and then we will quickly find the way." The moon soon shone forth, and Hansel, taking his sister's hand, followed the pebbles, which glittered like new-coined silver pieces, and showed them the path. All night long they walked on, and as day broke they came to their father's house. They knocked at the door, and when the wife opened it, and saw Hansel and Grethel, she exclaimed, "You wicked children! why did you sleep so long in the wood? We thought you were never coming home again." But their father was very glad, for it had grieved his heart to leave them all alone.

Not long afterwards there was again great scarcity in every corner of the land; and one night the children overheard their mother saying to their father, "Everything is again consumed; we have only half a loaf left, and then the song is ended: the children must be sent away. We will take them deeper into the wood, so that they may not find the way out again; it is the only means of escape for us."

But her husband felt heavy at heart, and thought, "It were better to share the last crust with the children." His wife, however, would listen to nothing that he said, and scolded and reproached him without end. He who says A must say B too; and he who consents the first time must also the second.

The children, however, had heard the conversation as they lay awake, and as soon as the old people went to sleep Hansel got up, intending to pick up some pebbles as before; but the wife had locked the door, so that he could not get out. Nevertheless he comforted Grethel, saying, "Do not cry; sleep in quiet; the good God will not forsake us."

Early in the morning the stepmother came and pulled them out of bed, and gave them each a slice of bread, which was still smaller than the former piece. On the way, Hansel broke his in his pocket, and, stooping every now and then, dropped a crumb upon the path. "Hansel, why do you stop and look about?" said the father, "keep in the path." "I am looking at my little dove," answered Hansel, "nodding a good-bye to me." "Simpleton!" said the wife, "that is no dove, but only the sun shining on the chimney." But Hansel kept still dropping crumbs as he went along.

Back into the Forest

The mother led the children deep into the wood, where they had never been before, and there making an immense fire, she said to them, "sit down here and rest, and when you feel tired you can sleep for a little while. We are going into the forest to hew wood, and in the evening, when we are ready, we will come and fetch you."

When noon came Grethel shared her bread with Hansel, who had strewn his on the path. Then they went to sleep; but the evening arrived and no one came to visit the poor children, and in the dark night they awoke, and Hansel comforted his sister by saying, "Only wait, Grethel, till the moon comes out, then we shall see the crumbs of bread which I have dropped, and they will show us the way home." The moon shone and they got up, but they could not see any crumbs, for the thousands of birds which had been flying about in the woods and fields had picked them all up. Hansel kept saying to Grethel, "We will soon find the way;" but they did not, and they walked the whole night long and the next day, but still they did not come out of the wood; and they got so hungry, for they had nothing to eat but the berries which they found upon the bushes. Soon they got so tired that they could not drag themselves along, so they lay down under a tree and went to sleep.

It was now the third morning since they had left their father's house and they still walked on; but they only got deeper and deeper into the wood, and Hansel saw that if help did not come very soon they would die of hunger. As soon as it was noon they saw a beautiful snow-white bird sitting upon a bough, which sang so sweetly that they stood still and listened to it. It soon left off, and spreading its wings flew off; and they followed it until it arrived at a cottage, upon the roof of which it perched; and when they went close up to it they saw that the cottage was made of bread and cakes, and the window-panes were of clear sugar.

The Old Woman

"We will go in there," said Hansel, "and have a glorious feast. I will eat a piece of the roof, and you can eat the window. Will they not be sweet?" So Hansel reached up and broke a piece off the roof, in order to see how it tasted; while Grethel stepped up to the window and began to bite it. Then a sweet voice called out in the room, "Tip-tap, tip-tap, who raps at my door?" and the children answered, "The wind, the wind, the child of heaven;" and they went on eating without interruption. Hansel thought the roof tasted very nice, and so he tore off a great piece, while Grethel broke a large round pane out of the window, and sat down quite contentedly. Just then the door opened, and a very old woman walking upon crutches, came out. Hansel and Grethel were so frightened that they let fall what they had in their hands; but the old woman, nodding her head, said, "Ah, you dear children, what has brought you here? Come in and stop with me, and no harm shall befall you;" and so saying she took them both by the hand, and led them into her cottage. A good meal of milk and pancakes, with sugar, apples, and nuts, was spread on the table, and in the back room were two nice little beds, covered with white, where Hansel and Grethel laid themselves down, and thought themselves in heaven. The old woman behaved very kindly to them, but in reality she was a wicked witch who waylaid children, and built the bread house in order to entice them in; but as soon as they were in her power she killed them, cooked and ate them, and made a great festival of the day. Witches have red eyes, and cannot see very far; but they have a fine sense of smelling, like wild beasts, so that they know when children approach them. When Hansel and Grethel came near the witch's house she laughed wickedly, saying, "Here come two who shall not escape me." And early in the morning, before they awoke, she went up to them, and saw how lovingly they lay sleeping, with their chubby red cheeks; and she mumbled to herself, "That will be a good bite." Then she took up Hansel with her rough hand, and shut him up in a little cage with a lattice-door; and although he screamed loudly it was of no use. Grethel came next, and, shaking her till she awoke, she said, "Get up, you lazy thing, and fetch some water to cook something good for your brother who must remain in that stall and get fat; when he is fat enough I shall eat him." Grethel began to cry, but it was all useless, for the old witch made her do as she wished. So a nice meal was cooked for Hansel, but Grethel got nothing else but a crab's claw.

Every morning the old witch came to the cage and said, "Hansel, stretch out your finger that I may feel whether you are getting fat." But Hansel used to stretch out a bone, and the old woman, having very bad sight, thought it was his finger, and wondered very much that he did not get more fat. When four weeks had passed, and Hansel, still kept quite lean, she lost all her patience, and would not wait any longer. "Grethel," she called out in a passion, "get some water quickly; be Hansel fat or lean, this morning I will kill and cook him." Oh, how the poor little sister grieved, as she was forced to fetch the water, and fast the tears ran down her cheeks! "Dear good God, help us now!" she exclaimed. "Had we only been eaten by the wild beasts in the wood, then we should have died together." But the old witch called out, "Leave off that noise; it will not help you a bit."

So early in the morning Grethel was forced to go out and fill the kettle, and make a fire. "First, we will bake, however," said the old woman; "I have already heated the oven and kneaded the dough;" and so saying, she pushed poor Grethel up to the oven, out of which the flames were burning fiercely. "Creep in," said the witch, "and see if it is hot enough, and then we will put in the bread; but she intended when Grethel got in to shut up the oven and let her bake, so that she might eat her as well as Hansel. Grethel perceived what her thoughts were, and said, "I do not know how to do it; how shall I get in?" "You stupid goose," said she, "the opening is big enough. See, I could even get in myself!" and she got up, and put her head into the oven. Then Grethel gave her a push, so that she fell right in, and then shutting the iron door she bolted it. Oh! how horribly she howled; but Grethel ran away, and left the ungodly witch to burn to ashes.

A Happy Ending

Now she ran to Hansel, and, opening his door, called out, "Hansel, we are saved; the old witch is dead!" So he sprang out, like a bird out of his cage when the door is opened; and they were so glad that they fell upon each other's neck, and kissed each other over and over again. And now, as there was nothing to fear, they went into the witch's house, where in every corner were caskets full of pearls and precious stones. "These are better than pebbles," said Hansel, putting as many into his pocket as it would hold; while Grethel thought, "I will take some home too," and filled her apron full. "We must be off now," said Hansel, "and get out of this enchanted forest;" but when they had walked for two hours they came to a large piece of water. "We cannot get over," said Hansel; "I can see no bridge at all." "And there is no boat either," said Grethel, "but there swims a white duck, I will ask her to help us over," and she sang,

> Little Duck, good little Duck,
>> Grethel and Hansel, here we stand;
> There is neither stile nor bridge,
>> Take us on your back to land.

So the Duck came to them, and Hansel sat himself on, and bade his sister sit behind him. "No," answered Grethel, "that will be too much for the Duck, she shall take us over one at a time." This the good little bird did, and when both were happily arrived on the other side, and had gone a little way, they came to a well-known wood, which they knew the better every step they went, and at last they perceived their father's house. Then they began to run, and, bursting into the house, they fell on their father's neck. He had not had one happy hour since he had left the children in the forest: and his wife was dead. Grethel shook her apron, and the pearls and precious stones rolled out upon the floor, and Hansel threw down one handful after the other out of his pocket. Then all their sorrows were ended, and they lived together in great happiness.

10

The Congress of Vienna Changes the Territorial Boundaries of Europe

by Charles W. Kegley Jr. and Gregory A. Raymond

In early 1814, the invasion of France by the Sixth Coalition (allied powers)—Great Britain, Austria, Prussia (Germany), Russia, and Sweden—brought the empire of Napoléon Bonaparte to an end. The emperor was forced to abdicate on April 6, 1814, and was exiled to the island of Elba. On May 30, 1814, the Treaty of Paris was signed. In addition to restoring the Bourbon dynasty to the throne in France, it called for a congress to be held in Vienna. The Congress of Vienna, the purpose of which was to stabilize a post-Napoleonic Europe, officially opened on October 1, 1814.

The objectives of the diplomats at Vienna included restructuring territory and restoring a balance of power to Europe. France, according to the Treaty of Paris, had to relinquish all territory it had gained as a result of Napoléon's wars. This resulted in the redrawing of numerous European borders. In addition, the European powers opted for monarchical governments throughout the continent in an effort to preserve order.

Charles W. Kegley Jr. and Gregory A. Raymond, *From War to Peace: Fateful Decisions in International Politics*. Boston: Bedford/St. Martin's Press, 2002. Copyright © 2002 by Bedford. Reproduced by permission of Wadsworth Publishing.

When Napoléon escaped from Elba in March 1815 and arrived in Paris, the Congress of Vienna was still taking place. Napoléon's return prompted quick action, though, and the documents devised were signed on June 9, 1815—just nine days prior to the former emperor's final defeat at the Battle of Waterloo.

In the following selection, Charles W. Kegley Jr. and Gregory A. Raymond present an explanation of the issues sorted out at the Congress of Vienna. They depict the political atmosphere in the wake of Napoléon. The authors also elaborate on both the points of agreement and those of contention among the powers.

Charles W. Kegley Jr. is peace professor of international relations at Syracuse University. He is also the author of over three dozen books. Gregory A. Raymond is director of the Honors College at Boise State University. He has published ten books and numerous articles on international relations.

N apoleon's defeat at Waterloo concluded a period that had battered Europe for almost a quarter century and left over 2.5 million combatants dead. When measured by battle deaths per population, the toll exceeded all previous wars fought during the preceding three centuries. The carnage inspired pity in people of compassion and horror in people of prudence. It galvanized a consensus among the victors who met at the Congress of Vienna about the need to prevent another great-power death struggle from again erupting.

Restoring a Conservative World

Vienna was famed for its charm and beauty. As the site for the peace deliberations, it played host to a dazzling assemblage of people: monarchs and their servants, diplomats and their deputies, generals and their aides, as well as wives, mistresses, spies, pickpockets, and hangers-on. Numerous banquets, teas, and balls were organized to delight the city's guests. Despite being almost bankrupt, the Austrians spent over 15 million dollars providing entertainment. Among the cultural events was the first performance by the German musician Beethoven of his Seventh Symphony.

While the festivities went on, statesmen toiled over more than just ending the roar of artillery. As the Austrian chancellor Prince Klemens von Metternich proclaimed in an opening session, the

Congress of Vienna had as its mission goals beyond those of previous peace congresses.

> It does not require any great political insight to see that this Congress could not model itself on any predecessor. Previous meetings which have been called congresses have confined themselves to making treaties of peace between parties which were either at war or ready to go to war. This time the treaty of peace is already made, and the parties are meeting as friends, not necessarily having the same interests, who wish to work together to complete and affirm the existing Treaty. The matters to be negotiated are a multifarious list of questions, in some cases partly settled by previous discussions, in other cases, as yet untouched. The Powers which made the Treaty of Paris will determine the meaning which they wish to attach to the word Congress, and will also decide the form which would seem most appropriate for reaching the goals they have set themselves. They will use this right of determination equally to the advantage of the interested parties, and thus, to the good of Europe as a whole, and the plenipotentiaries at Vienna will deal with matters in the most efficient, prompt and confidential way. Thus the Congress is brought into being of itself, without having received any formal authority, there being no source which could have given any.

The victors in the Napoleonic Wars operated from an unusually high level of agreement about the rules that should govern their future relations. The world they restored was a conservative world defined with an unusual clarity of purpose and consistency of vision. Napoleon's quest for hegemony had challenged not only the existing distribution of power on the European continent, but also the self-help system of legitimized competition among sovereign great-power equals that policymakers inspired by realist theory advocated. Napoleon embraced an imperial vision of international order with himself at the apex of authority; he had tried to recreate the quasi-world government that had operated throughout the medieval system prior to the 1648 Peace of Westphalia. But with the defeat of Napoleon came the defeat of his vision for a new international order. Metternich, backed by Russian czar Alexander I, Prussian king Frederick William III, and British foreign minister Castlereagh, tried to restore as much of the pre-Napoleonic map of Europe as possible and return to the laissez-faire rules so that the old Westphalian game could be played again.

Balance of Power

The bargains struck among the victorious powers about territorial matters reflected the realpolitik belief that conflict was a natural component of interstate interaction. Disputes were bound to arise just as friction results from objects in contact. Whereas they might not be able to prevent future disputes, realist leaders assumed that they could reduce the likelihood of such disputes escalating to war by preserving an equilibrium among the great powers. In effect, the final act of the peace settlement of the Congress of Vienna re-drew the map of Europe, guided not just by the goal of rewarding the victors for their sacrifices, but, more importantly, of making Austria, Russia, Prussia, Great Britain, and France approximately equal in their capacity to wage war. A stable balance of power was sought, with territorial boundaries altered so that no single state would be in a position to threaten the rest.

To attain this goal, the negotiators bargained long and hard to delineate a new set of borders that would allow the invisible hand of the balance of power to work. The biggest prize went to Russia, as Poland was again partitioned with the czar gaining the largest slice. Russia also received Finland from Sweden, which had gained Norway from Denmark. To build a counterweight to France, Prussia gained a portion of Saxony, all the German territories Napoleon had taken from it, as well as land in Westphalia and the Rhineland. For similar reasons, Austria regained the Tyrol and other formerly held land, including territories in wealthy and strategically important regions of Italy, as compensation for its willingness to accept the suspension of claims on the southern Netherlands. The Vienna settlement also permitted the Vatican's recovery of its former possessions in central Italy, and Switzerland was made a neutral state. In addition to these and other changes in Europe, modifications were made in colonial possessions, again with the aim of fine-tuning the overall equilibrium. For example, Great Britain returned to the Netherlands all the overseas territories seized in 1806, except for Ceylon, the Cape Colony in Africa, and part of the Guyana coast of South America east of Venezuela. In compensation, the various settlements on the Atlantic coast (including the colonies of the Essequibo River, Berbice, and Demerara) were united in 1831 to form the Crown Colony of British Guiana, the only British colony in South America.

Not Liberty but Peace

The most memorable aspect of the peace settlement was its resuscitative policy toward the defeated power, France, which had tried to establish universal dominion. Article 32 of the first Treaty of Paris provided for French representation at Vienna, but a secret clause excluded France from the actual decision making. However, Charles-Maurice de Talleyrand, who represented France at the congress, was able to use discord among the victors to leverage French participation in the negotiations. France, it was finally concluded, would be needed as a balancer to help police the new order, and its exclusion, partition, or forced demise could easily become the seed of a subsequent war. A conciliatory attitude toward France was seen as prudent because a Bourbon government in Paris could help shore up monarchical rule elsewhere in Europe.

Talleyrand's appeals to the "sacred principle of monarchical legitimacy" helped to prevent his nation from remaining a pariah. The former bishop of Auteuil, who had forsaken the Catholic Church during the Revolution only to abandon the Revolution for Napoleon, was famous for his caustic wit and cleverness. It was said that he had both the laughers and the thinkers on his side. Upon arriving in Vienna, he insisted that with Napoleon gone, the victors had no right to exclude Bourbon France from the deliberations. His reiteration of the mantra of legitimacy eventually resonated with conservatives, who feared the Continent might suffer a relapse into revolutionary turmoil. As Metternich put it, what Europe wanted was not liberty but peace.

Organizing Collective Responses

To maintain peace after the congress ended, the diplomats in Vienna established the Concert of Europe, an oligarchic system of great-power consultation and policy coordination. The assumption behind the concert was that discussion and consensus building among those at the apex of the global hierarchy would produce multilateral decision making on divisive issues. Compromise and collaboration, rather than the thrust and parry of unbridled competition, would yield outcomes acceptable to all of the great powers. Not only would rule by this self-appointed coalition help control rivalries among the mighty, but it would provide a vehicle for enforcing peace among the smaller states, whose conflicts and civil wars could draw the great powers into combat.

Although theorists had in earlier times advocated various organizational schemes for orchestrating such collective responses to common problems, none were ever implemented. What made the climate of early-nineteenth-century opinion different was shared great-power fear of the strife unleashed by the French Revolution. Democratic ideals had taken root in a political landscape populated by monarchies adhering to strict realist conceptions of rules for peacekeeping. The consequences for European royalty were profound:

Decision makers no longer felt more loyalty to each other than to their own people. Fewer social and cultural ties united decision makers of different countries, and correspondingly more social and cultural ties grew between each country's decision makers and its general populace. The willingness to use more force and less restraint against other states increased as members of the system became geographically dispersed and culturally heterogeneous. Increases in speed of transportation and communication did more to tie nations together internally than promoting cooperation among states. Xenophobia, the fear and hatred of foreign states, became a force . . . in almost every state. Where [before the French Revolution] the classical decision maker had difficulty in engendering patriotism among nations, the decision maker [after the French Revolution] had difficulty in controlling patriotism in order to follow a flexible foreign policy.

From this setting emerged a set of rules that took a different posture toward the use of force than had existed in the seventeenth century. Intervention in the internal affairs of states, for example, was uncommon in the eighteenth century; but since revolutionary France had overturned the constitutions of conservative states, reactionary statesmen like Metternich and Friedrich Gentz now proclaimed the right to use forcible methods to suppress revolutionary uprisings within other nations' borders. United in a common cause to combat rebellion from within, the victors experimented with the idea of collective intervention. For instance, at the Congress of Aix-la-Chapelle in 1818, Czar Alexander I of Russia proposed an alliance to intervene on behalf of rulers who were threatened by insurrection.

Elusive Unanimity

However, great-power unanimity proved to be elusive. While the British were willing to help the three Eastern monarchies stem military aggression aimed at overturning the post-Napoleonic balance of power, they did not countenance military intervention to prop up tottering autocrats. Foreign Minister Castlereagh, for example, refused Metternich's invitation in 1819 to approve the Carlsbad Decree and in 1829 rejected the Protocol of Troppau. In the first instance, the burning of conservative books and the murder of a conservative journalist by members of the German nationalist student movement prompted Metternich to convene a meeting of the larger German states at Carlsbad, where he coerced those leaders to promulgate measures he had drafted in order to suppress liberal nationalist ideas. In the second instance, revolts in Spain and Naples led the three Eastern courts to agree at the Congress of Troppau that force could be used against states that had been transformed by internal upheaval and were threatening to their neighbors. Although Castlereagh was sympathetic to the fears held by his counterparts across the Channel, he resisted the use of the congress system to regulate other states' domestic affairs. Castlereagh, observed the Austrian ambassador in London, "is like a great lover of music who is at church; he wishes to applaud but he dares not."

Despite British refusal to police sociopolitical disturbances, Austria, Prussia, and Russia were determined to use the Concert of Europe to prevent revolution. Therefore, at the Congress of Laibach the three conservative powers sanctioned Austria's intervention into Naples and Piedmont to suppress liberal revolts, and the following year at Verona they agreed to a French proposal to crush rebels in Spain.

Napoléon's Final Defeat Takes Place at the Battle of Waterloo: June 18, 1815

Waterloo Gave Britain Confidence

by Rory Muir

Napoléon's defeat in the spring of 1814 effected the abdication and exile of the French emperor. Sent to the island of Elba, Napoléon was disenchanted with his banishment from the start. In the meantime, he kept informed about the Congress of Vienna and learned that the allied powers were divided over some territorial issues. He schemed to escape from Elba, hoping to exploit this split and wage war against the allies while they were at odds with one another.

Napoléon's return is called the "Hundred Days." It began on March 20, 1815, when he arrived in Paris. There he gathered an army and launched an attack against the allies, who put aside their disagreements to unite against him. Arthur Wellesley, Duke of Wellington, led the British-German forces to victory over Napoléon at Waterloo on June 18, 1815. The end of the Hundred Days is June 28, 1815, when King Louis XVIII was again restored. Napoléon was imprisoned for life on the remote island of St. Helena, where he remained until his death in 1821.

In the following excerpt, Rory Muir provides details about the complicated Battle of Waterloo. He describes what happened in France after Waterloo, both militarily and politically. Muir also elaborates on the fate of Napoléon and the legacy of Waterloo in Great Britain.

Historian Rory Muir is a visiting research fellow at the University of Southampton in England. He is the author of several books on the Napoleonic era.

Rory Muir, *Britain and the Defeat of Napoleon, 1807–1815*. New Haven, CT: Yale University Press, 1996. Copyright © 1996 by Rory Muir. All rights reserved. Reproduced by permission.

Contemporary accounts of the battle certainly make confusing reading, and it was many years before the now familiar story, with its orderly succession of events and the different phases of the French attack, emerged. Modern accounts still follow this model, and they are probably as accurate as it is possible to be and remain comprehensible, but it is nonetheless likely that they involve a good deal of oversimplification and that the reality was much more confused than they make it appear.

A Confusing Battle

According to the accepted account, the battle began about 11.30 A.M. with the French artillery bombarding the centre of the allied line and, shortly afterwards, an infantry attack on Hougoumont which continued all day without any success. D'Erlon's corps then advanced to attack the left centre of the British position, i.e. La Haye Sainte and the ground to the east of the Charleroi-Brussels highway. Bijlandt's Dutch-Belgian brigade, which had been left exposed on the forward slope of the ridge, took flight; but the French were then repulsed in great disorder by Picton's division and the charge of the British heavy cavalry (the Union and Household brigades), including the Scots Greys. As was their besetting fault, the British cavalry got out of hand and went too far, and then suffered great loss when the French cavalry reserves advanced against them and forced them to fall back to their original position. A pause now followed while both sides collected and reorganized their forces. The French artillery continued to bombard the allied line, inflicting considerable casualties, despite the protection afforded by being on the reverse slope. Fighting continued at Hougoumont and at La Haye Sainte, and Napoleon began to take serious precautions to protect his right flank and rear from the Prussians. (Leading elements of Bülow's corps had first been observed in the middle of the morning, but due to the long march and difficult nature of the countryside the corps spread back for miles, and it was the middle of the afternoon before sufficient troops were collected to advance further.) Ney now led succession of cavalry charges against the right centre of Wellington's line (between Hougoumont and La Haye Sainte). The allied infantry formed squares and repulsed the attacks but suffered greatly from the French artillery, while by the close of this stage of the battle the French cavalry were a spent force. Late in the afternoon or in the early evening, La Haye Sainte fell when its King's German Legion garrison finally ran out of ammunition. From this secure post the French poured a withering fire into the centre of the allied line. Wellington was running short of reserves, and it is sometimes argued that if Napoleon had made his final attack then, he would have carried the day. But the Prussians were advancing through Placenoit and threatening the French rear. Napoleon had already committed first Lobau's corps, and then the Young Guard, to check their advance, which had succeeded for a time, but now they were again being driven back. He drew on his ultimate reserve and committed two battalions of the Old Guard to the struggle, and they recaptured Placenoit and stabilized this front again. But the pause had given Wellington time to rally his forces. Zieten's troops now protected the British left flank, releasing the light cavalry brigades of Vivian and Vandeleur to strengthen the allied centre. The details of the final French attack, led by the Grenadiers and Chasseurs of the Imperial Guard, have been the subject of endless controversy, and many a British officer brightened the long years of retirement on half pay by maintaining, in pamphlets and the columns of Colburn's *United Service Magazine*, that the principal credit for the defeat of the famous Imperial Guard rested with his regiment and his regiment alone. Whoever was right, the Guard fell back in disorder. Napoleon's last reserves were gone, Wellington ordered a general advance all along the line, and the French army broke and fled in confusion. The Prussians took over the pursuit, Blücher and Wellington met, possibly at the inn named La Belle Alliance (though Wellington later denied it, and the story seems too good to be true), and Napoleon barely escaped capture in the rout.

The losses suffered by the armies show the intensity of the fighting at Waterloo. While estimates vary, it seems likely that the French lost at least 30,000 casualties in the battle and about 7,000 unwounded prisoners. Many French regiments appear to have lost more than half their strength. Wellington's army lost more than 15,000 men, of whom about half were British, while the Prussians lost nearly 7,000. Thus 50,000 men were killed or wounded in a few square miles on that single day, along with perhaps 10,000 horses. Wellington was shaken by the losses, which included Sir Thomas Picton, killed at the head of his troops, and Lord Uxbridge who, famously, lost his leg at the very end of the battle, while many of Wellington's own staff had been either killed or wounded. He wrote to the Duke of Beaufort, whose brother, Fitzroy Somerset, was seriously wounded, 'the losses I have sustained have quite broken me down, and I have no feeling for the advantages we have acquired'. And he told Lord Aberdeen, whose brother Alexander Gordon had been killed, 'The glory resulting from such actions, so dearly bought, is no consolation to me, and I cannot suggest it as any to you and his friends'. . . .

After Waterloo

After Waterloo the allied armies advanced into France, meeting little resistance. Napoleon's army was utterly shattered, and though Grouchy was able to extricate his force in a skilful retreat, the war was clearly lost. Napoleon hurried to Paris, but once there hesitated over what to do. He could have dissolved the assembly, imposed martial law, and attempted to rally the army and the people against the allied invasion; but this offered no real prospect of success, his will to resist was broken, and on 22 June [1815] he abdicated in favour of his son. A provisional government was appointed, including Fouché, Caulaincourt and Carnot, and on 24 June it asked Wellington and Blücher, whose forces were advancing on Paris, for an armistice. Both generals refused and continued their advance, but contact was maintained and on 29 June Wellington informed the French commissioners, 'before I could stop my operations, I must see some steps taken to re-establish a government in France which should afford the Allies some chance of peace'. When pressed to explain what would satisfy the allies, he denied that he had any authority to speak on the subject, but then informed them that his personal opinion was that

> the best security for Europe was the restoration of the King, and that the establishment of any other government than the King's in France must inevitably lead to new and endless wars; that Buonaparte and the army having overturned the King's government, the simple and natural measure, after Buonaparte was prisoner or out of the way, and the army defeated, was to recall the King to his authority, and that it was a much more dignified proceeding to recall him without conditions, and to trust to the energy of their constitution for any reforms they wished to make either in the government or the constitution, than now to make conditions with their Sovereign; and that, above all, it was important that they should recall the King without loss of time, as it would not then appear that the measure had been forced upon them by the Allies.

Wellington went on explicitly to rule out allied acceptance of Napoleon II and to indicate his personal opposition to the Duc d'Orléans. He exchanged letters and had several meetings with Fouché, and the two men got on remarkably well, with Wellington continuing to champion Fouché's interests well after the restoration had been achieved. And while Fouché managed the actual transition in Paris, it was largely owing to Wellington's bluntness that the allies and the Bourbons were spared any serious intrigue to support an alternative government.

Paris formally capitulated on 3 July. The British and Prussian armies occupied the barriers on the 6th and entered the city on the following day, with Louis XVIII arriving on the 8th, one hundred and eleven days after he had fled in the night. Wellington reported that the city was 'perfectly quiet', but later there were such reports of enthusiasm that Bathurst commented, 'they are quite wild with rapture at having been conquered again'. The French army withdrew behind the Loire, and Marshal Davout struggled hard to keep it in order, hoping to demand concessions from the new regime, including an amnesty for all political offences committed during Napoleon's return and a pledge that the army would not be purged. The government, however, would not negotiate and the troops deserted in large numbers, leaving Davout with no choice but to make his submission to the King on 14 July.

The Convention of Paris contained a clause promising immunity to the citizens for their past political behaviour, and this raised concern in London that it might be construed as a general amnesty. Wellington replied by pointing out that the Convention only bound the parties to it, that is the allied armies, but could not hinder the French government from prosecuting traitors. The British government was extremely anxious for Louis XVIII to do so, Liverpool arguing that the restored regime could only establish its authority by showing that it dared to spill blood. 'It is a curious circumstance,' he told Canning, 'that after the sanguinary scenes which we recollect at the beginning of the French Revolution, all parties appear now to have an insuperable repugnance to executions. This arises not from mercy, but from fear'. Liverpool's diagnosis was true of Paris, but not some of the provinces, where ultra-royalist mobs were soon taking vengeance on their local Bonapartist opponents in what has been called the 'White Terror'. Such behaviour appalled Talleyrand, Fouché and other 'liberal' ministers in Louis XVIII's first government, and it was only considerable pressure both from the allies and from the royalists that produced a list of fifty-seven exclusions from the general amnesty issued by the King. Fouché, who was still Minister of Police despite being at least as guilty as any of the fifty-seven, ensured that they all received ample warning and opportunities to escape. Only three were arrested and tried, Marshal Ney, General La Bédoyère and Count Lavalette, but they were all sentenced to death. This produced an outcry among the Whigs in England, and Sir Robert Wilson helped Lavalette to escape, but La Bédoyère and Ney were shot by firing squads in August and December. And so the intrepid Michel Ney, the most heroic and probably the most popular of all the marshals, died in the end at the hands of French soldiers.

What to Do with Napoleon

The great outstanding problem of this kind was what to do with Napoleon, and here too the experience of 1814 warned against leniency. Blücher favoured a summary execution if the ex-Emperor should be captured by Prussian troops, but Wellington urged him 'to have nothing to do with so foul a transaction', and argued, 'that he [Blücher] and I had acted too distinguished parts in these transactions to become executioners; and that I was determined that if the Sovereigns wished to put him to death they should appoint an executioner, which should not be me'. But Wellington had no wish to see Napoleon go free and refused to give him passports to the United States, as did the British admiral off Rochefort where Napoleon had taken refuge. Seeing that there was no hope of escape, the fugitive Emperor surrendered to Captain Maitland of H.M.S. *Bellerophon* on 16 July, sending the Prince Regent a grandiloquent appeal:

> Exposed to the factions which distract my country and to the enmity of the greatest powers of Europe, I have closed my political career, and I come, like Themistocles, to throw myself upon the hospitality of the British people. I put myself under the protection of their laws, which I claim from your Royal Highness, as the most powerful, the most constant, and the most generous of my enemies.

This blatant appeal to the Regent's vanity caused much comment and discussion in England, with one wag suggesting that it would earn Napoleon the Garter at least, while Lady Holland was reported to be 'very cross and absurd about Buonaparte, "poor dear man", as she calls him'.

The *Bellerophon* brought Napoleon to England, but he was not allowed to land, and huge crowds of spectators thronged out in small boats to catch a glimpse of him; some were passionately enthusiastic, others merely curious. Sir Francis Burdett had to be dissuaded by Romilly from moving a writ of habeas corpus for Napoleon's release; and a subpoena was actually issued requiring Napoleon's testimony in a libel case in London—a manoeuvre which was only defeated by Lord Keith and the *Bellerophon* making strenuous efforts to avoid the man who came to serve the subpoena. In general, though, the mood of the country was still very hostile to Napoleon, an attitude encouraged by a virulent press full of cheap abuse and derisive jeers. The ministers felt little sympathy or sentiment for their fallen opponent, and Croker's reaction to Napoleon's appeal probably expresses the most common reaction of country and cabinet alike:

> I could not help bursting out into a loud laugh, which astonished the French, who thought all beautiful, but *'Thémistocle'* sublime and pathetic. I called the whole letter a base flattery, and said Buonaparte should have died rather than have written such a one; the only proper answer to it would have been to have enclosed him a copy of one of his *Moniteurs*, in which he accused England of assassination and every other horror.

The government still had to decide what to do with their troublesome prisoner. With some exasperation Liverpool told Castlereagh, 'we wish that the King of France would hang or shoot Bonaparte as the best termination of the business', but this was clearly no longer practical, and Liverpool may not have been altogether serious. The allies were happy to let Britain take charge of the prisoner, and Castlereagh suggested that he be detained in a fortress in Scotland, but Liverpool objected. There were legal difficulties with detaining him in Great Britain and he would attract too much public attention, and in any case it was desirable to send him far away, so that his presence would no longer 'contribute to keep up a certain degree of ferment in France'. So the decision was taken to send him to St Helena, a small island in the middle of the South Atlantic, with a healthy climate, and which was secure enough to enable him to live with a reasonable degree of freedom. The story of his unhappy exile and descent into petty quarrels with the Governor, which exacerbated his rapidly deteriorating health, is too well known to need repeating here. And while we may regret that the British government did not act with greater generosity, particularly on small points of little consequence which touched the Emperor's pride, we must recognize that its prime responsibility was to help establish and maintain the peace and stability of the new European settlement which Napoleon had already once disrupted. . . .

Importance of Waterloo

How important was Waterloo? Few battles are so immediately decisive, with a war being won on a single bloody afternoon. Yet if Napoleon had won, would history have been very different? It has become customary to say that it mattered little who won the battle, and that even if Napoleon had triumphed he would soon have been overthrown by the vast Austrian and Russian armies which were gathering against him. Perhaps so, but there seems little reason for confidence on such a hypothetical question. If Napoleon had defeated Wellington and Blücher, he might well have gone on to defeat the Russians and Austrians, and even consolidate his power permanently in France. The odds would still have been against him, but they were rapidly shortening. And only those who view the past in quasi-geological terms—happily taking the long view of 500 years, where no individuals matter much—can fairly argue that Napoleon's success or failure was of little consequence.

But there is another sense in which Waterloo is important, for as well as being a French defeat, it was a British victory, the crowning glory which brought the long war to a fitting close. The war as a whole, and Waterloo in particular, gave Britain a sense of uniqueness, an inner confidence, which lasted a full century until it was shattered on the Somme. Alone of the European powers, she had withstood the whirlwind unleashed by the French Revolution unscathed. French troops had never marched in triumph through London as they had through Vienna, Rome, Madrid, Lisbon, Brussels, Amsterdam, Berlin, Warsaw and Moscow. Britain had not tasted the bitter humiliation of defeat and had prospered while her allies had collapsed. In 1783, only ten years before the war began, Britain had been defeated and divided by the American war; now that memory was expunged, not only by the victory over France, but by the defeat of the United States in the war of 1812. The loss of the American colonies had been offset by the acquisition of a new colonial empire, and by unprecedented dominance of international trade and the high seas. Waterloo set the seal on this achievement. Britain triumphed on land, as she had long done on the sea, and had overthrown the all-conquering enemy. Popular memory soon forgot Napoleon's first abdication: Waterloo was the last and greatest of Sir Edward Creasy's *Fifteen Decisive Battles of the World*, while eighty years after the battle an Australian clergyman expressed the mood of the time when he called his four-volume history of the French wars *How England Saved Europe.*

Nelson and Trafalgar, Moore and Coruña, Wellington and Waterloo, thus became the focus for popular British patriotism throughout the nineteenth century. The war and its memory gave the British people a taste for military glory and greatly eroded the traditional distrust of standing armies.

12

Repatriated Slaves Sail for Liberia:
February 6, 1820

The Hope for a Black Homeland

by Floyd J. Miller

In 1816 the American Colonization Society (ACS) was founded to promote a colonization plan that would enable freed slaves to settle in Africa. Congress appropriated one hundred thousand dollars to aid the private organization. On February 6, 1820, eighty-eight former slaves and three ACS members set sail on the *Elizabeth* from New York to West Africa. The first attempt to settle was unsuccessful; twenty-two of the emigrants and the three ACS agents died from yellow fever. The initial settlement on an island off the Sierra Leone coast was only temporary, and several other sites were visited on the continent before a permanent place was obtained. After a few negotiations and the arrival of more emigrants, Dr. Eli Ayres of the ACS and Lieutenant Robert Stockton of the U.S. Navy purchased land in 1821. The land constitutes modern Liberia, which became an official settlement in 1822. Because President James Monroe assisted the land arrangement, the capital city of Monrovia is named after him.

In the following excerpt, Floyd J. Miller addresses the issue of black emigration in the context of repatriation. He discusses the foundation of Liberia and the reaction of freed blacks and abolitionists to the idea of colonization. Miller also reflects on the motivations and goals of black emigrants, as well as the overall impact of the colonization movement in the pre–Civil War period.

Floyd J. Miller is the author of several books on black history.

Floyd J. Miller, *The Search for Black Nationality: Black Emigration and Colonization 1787–1863*. Chicago: University of Illinois Press, 1975. Copyright © 1975 by Floyd J. Miller. Reproduced by permission.

L eaving home to seek one's fortune in other parts has usually stirred up a multitude of conflicting emotions and loyalties.

Emigration as a Return

Partly a rejection of the emigrant's past, his native land, and even perhaps his family, emigration has also signified the hope of a future marked by economic prosperity, religious freedom, or political liberty. But for those Africans who were brought, enslaved and unwilling, across the Atlantic to a New World they never sought, emigration signified something very different. For these very first Africans in the British colonies, emigration was a return to, not a flight from, their homelands and their peoples—whether in Angola or Yoruba or Mandingo. Yet for their descendants, the Afro-Americans, the return "back to Africa," was very different: they could not go *back*, for they were no longer what their fathers were.

If no longer purely African, they were still, in their own eyes and in those of the whites who castigated them, very much *black* (African, yes; but much more and much less), and it was as Afro-Americans that they shaped a relationship with the land of their birth, but not of their people. Although from the late eighteenth century until the beginning of the Civil War most free blacks in the North accepted the consequences of this anomaly, a significant number of articulate and forceful free blacks called upon their fellow blacks in both the United States and Canada to flee to other lands and there begin a new future intertwined by necessity and destiny with that of their black brethren. Their motives varied, as did their destinations, and their voices were heeded by only a few of the relatively small number of politically involved blacks. But during most of the seventy-five years prior to the Civil War, black emigrationists reiterated their belief that only by leaving North America to join with blacks elsewhere could they ever free themselves from further oppression and degradation. . . .

African Colonization

The death of [blackship captain and emigrationist] Paul Cuffe [in 1817] and the formation of the American Colonization Society [in 1816] presented a dilemma for those blacks who had previously embraced emigration. In addition to losing their most effective and best-known advocate, they were confronted with a new symbol of repression. Whatever the exact mixture of benevolence and racism which characterized the Colonization Society at this time, most Afro-Americans viewed the organization as a deportation society whose members believed both in black inferiority and in the necessity of ridding the country of its free black population in order to preserve the institution of slavery. Nevertheless, some blacks worked with or endorsed the Society. There were those who decided that, regardless of the motives of the Colonization Society's members, planting an Afro-American colony in West Africa would free blacks from the degradation they experienced in the United States and present them with new social and economic opportunities. For others, the Colonization Society provided a means of transportation to Africa, enabling them to fulfill missionary ambitions. As a result, in the early 1820's several hundred black Americans with varying purposes emigrated to the colony of Liberia.

Moreover, not all blacks who rejected African colonization were opposed to emigration as such. For a number of these individuals emigration to a nearby black nation such as Haiti provided an alternative to suffering continued oppression at home. Indeed, encouraged by the Haitian government, several thousand blacks reportedly migrated to the Caribbean republic in 1824 and 1825. However, a large proportion of the emigrants quickly became dissatisfied with their new homes and returned to the United States.

Opposition to African colonization also revived following the collapse of the Haitian emigration movement; by the end of the decade it had broadened into a general attack upon all forms of emigration. In 1831 William Lloyd Garrison orchestrated numerous black protest meetings announcing that blacks would not leave the United States, and after 1833 the national black conventions (which met consecutively from 1830 through 1835) registered opposition to "all plans of colonization any where," while also denouncing the American Colonization Society.

Free from White Domination

When the Colonization Society announced in the fall of 1819 that it would be sending a party of blacks to Africa with the assistance of the federal government, several hundred would-be emigrants applied to the Society. Among those who eventually sailed from New York on the Society's maiden voyage in February, 1820, was the Reverend Daniel Coker, a Baltimore minister and formerly a supporter of Paul Cuffe's initial plan for a limited missionary-emigration to Africa. Not materially equipped to found their colony unassisted, the black settlers were compelled to depend upon both the Society and the federal government to a much greater extent than they had desired. Coker, caught between his friendship with the white agents who led the expedition and the increasingly independent black settlers, was at or near the center of the difficulties and tensions which dominated the two years between the departure of the first emigrants and the actual planting of the colony of Liberia at Cape Mesurado on the west coast of Africa. However, after the arrival in March, 1821, of a second emigrant vessel, Coker's pivotal role in the search for a colony was increasingly assumed by the Reverend Lott Cary, a Baptist missionary from Richmond, Virginia. Although Cary was initially an antagonist of the agents, his leadership was eventually recognized by both whites and blacks. Basically committed to preaching the Gospel to indigenous Africans, Cary also recognized what neither Coker nor the American Colonization Society ever understood: that the black American emigrants regarded the Society as a means of transporting them to a land where they hoped to live free from the intrusions of white domination.

Well before the Colonization Society's first group of emigrants departed from New York, its leaders had started to look for territory for the projected colony. In 1817 and 1818 Samuel J. Mills and Ebenezer Burgess, agents of the Society, had undertaken a "mission of inquiry" to England and Africa. Although Mills died before returning to the United States, Burgess arrived in the summer of 1818 ecstatic about Sherbro Island, the home of John Kizell, president of the Friendly Society and a man Mills had regarded as "a second Paul Cuffe." The island, Burgess reported, was "a land stored with the choicest minerals, bearing the richest fruits and covered with a profuse and luxuriant vegetation. . . ." With misleading optimism, he assured the Colonization Society that "the kings in Sherbro promised tracts of land . . . whenever any of the free people of colour might move thither." Letters Burgess brought back from members of the Friendly Society and from some of the emigrants Cuffe had carried to Sierra Leone also extolled the virtues of the Sherbro region. One of the early emigrants, Perry Lockes, argued that because "there is no man of colour that can say he is not ashamed in America," blacks should come to Africa and work for the conversion of the heathen Africans. Combining providential and materialistic tones, Lockes claimed that "it is the will of GOD for you to come into the possessions of your ancestors." Another emigrant who accompanied Cuffe, Samuel Wilson, heralded the economic advantages of Africa and maintained that his own personal fortune had grown from almost nothing when he arrived in Africa to a hundred pounds. Wilson also criticized the A.M.E. [African Methodist Episcopal] Church Bishop Richard Allen, who was now an unequivocal foe of African colonization. "When will you become a nation," Wilson finally queried, "if you refuse to come?"

Enlisting Emigrants

Whatever impact the publication of these letters in the United States may have had, blacks from various parts of the country began to respond to the Colonization Society's attempts to enlist emigrants for a projected expedition. From the Illinois Territory, one Abraham Camp wrote that a large number of free blacks living on the Wabash River were ready to go to Africa, for ". . . our freedom is partial, and we have no hope that it ever will be otherwise here; therefore, we had rather be gone, though we should suffer hunger and nakedness for years." By the spring of 1819 free blacks from the Wabash area had sold their lands and were waiting to leave for Africa. Significant numbers of blacks from most major cities in the North and South also wrote to the Colonization Society expressing their desire to migrate to Africa. At the same time, President Monroe bowed to the pressure of zealous colonizationists and decided that provisions of the Slave Trade Act of 1819 requiring the government to relocate recaptured Africans would allow cooperation with the Colonization Society. Financial aid would be provided to send to Africa black colonists who could also serve as government laborers constructing camps for the victims of the slave trade.

With federal funds now available and with applications from potential black colonists pouring into the Colonization Society's Washington office, there was no longer any reason to postpone the beginning of the colonization venture. In the fall of 1819 an agent for the Society chartered a 300-ton British-built vessel, the *Elizabeth*, for the trip to Africa, and the charter was quickly transferred to the government. As prospective emigrants began arriving in New York, the three whites scheduled to lead the expedition— Samuel Bacon and John Bankson, the government agents, and Samuel Crozer, acting for the Colonization Society—selected eighty-eight blacks. The agents never explained what criteria they used in choosing the emigrant party. . . .

Emigration Decline

Several factors contributed to the ante-bellum black emigrationists' inability to attract a larger following to their cause. For one thing, only a few Afro-Americans possessed the material resources necessary to emigrate, let alone succeed in another country. Second—as those who have downplayed the importance of ante-bellum emigration have argued—large numbers of blacks simply regarded themselves as more American than African. To many of these individuals, the United States possessed material advantages which far overshadowed the nation's harsh and oppressive treatment of its black inhabitants. Africa—or Haiti, for that matter—promised little but unrelenting toil and perhaps illness or death. Africa, too, for some of these people, was the physical presence of a degraded and barbarian past they wished to extirpate through neglect. Although other Afro-Americans were less critical of Africa and other locales in which blacks congregated, they believed that large-scale free black emigration from North America was, in effect, an abandoning of their brethren still enslaved as well a symbolic endorsement of white colonizationists who viewed deportation as a means of ridding the nation of people they considered inherently inferior.

Part of the explanation for the small number of free blacks who left North America—small even when one includes those blacks carried to Liberia under the auspices of the American Colonization Society—also rests with the sentiments of the black emigrationists themselves. As implied earlier, the emigrationists were unable to reach beyond the thin layer of middle-class blacks in the professions, small businesses, and skilled trades. In this respect they hardly differed from their opponents, for during the ante-bellum period few black laborers and domestic workers publicly embraced *any* political or social position. Many of the emigrationists, by renouncing general or mass emigration in favor of a more limited, "select" movement, actively excluded the participation of all but the educated, skilled, and propertied. In part, these emigrationists were attempting to answer those opponents who claimed that large-scale free black emigration would help preserve the institution of slavery in the southern states. Essentially, however, this rejection of mass emigration was integrally related to the moral reform and self-help ideology which permeated the thinking of most emigrationists.

Although the adoption of moral reform and self-help rhetoric certainly did not distinguish the emigrationists from other black activists of the ante-bellum period, in the context of emigrationism, the emphasis upon moral reform insured that the call for a limited emigration would indeed be heeded. Moral reformers in general held that blacks failing to achieve material success and respectability should be held personally accountable for their social and economic situation, but the exhortations of Delany, Lewis Woodson, and some of the other emigrationists contained especially harsh notes of paternalism and rebuke which could only have offended whatever black workers they may have reached. In addition, the writings of Cuffe, Holly, and other missionary-emigrationists were imbued with a sense of Christian righteousness which showed disdain for those whose lack of external accomplishments mirrored, so these emigrationists believed, an impure inner life. Finally, moral reform ideology sharply contradicted the basic assumptions of emigrationism, since self-help implied that moral conversion would inevitably enable blacks to overcome the larger social and economic problems they confronted. Of course, if this were the case, emigration from North America would be unnecessary.

However, despite the small number of free blacks who left the United States and Canada during the seventy-five years between the Constitutional Convention of 1787 and the unveiling of the Emancipation Proclamation, emigration was a strikingly resilient and pervasive element in the social and intellectual history of ante-bellum free blacks.

Repatriated Slaves Sail for Liberia:
February 6, 1820

Life in Liberia Is a Struggle

by Augustus Washington

The founding of Liberia in 1822 provoked controversy in the United States. Some abolitionists were critical of the American Colonization Society's actions. They claimed that repatriating freed slaves to Africa could actually reinforce proslavery arguments because the removal of free blacks implied that there was no place for them in American society. Overall, the free blacks themselves, some of whom were born in the United States to freed slaves, were not enthusiastic about going to Liberia.

Between 1820 and 1860, more than eleven thousand black emigrants were brought to Liberia. The country itself endured a tumultuous infrastructure and economic hardship, which made settling there a difficult and challenging transition. The United States had a tenuous relationship with the newly founded country. Nevertheless, Liberia remained a free country even when nearly all of Africa had been colonized by European powers in the late nineteenth century.

The following 1854 narrative by settler Augustus Washington, son of a former slave, documents his experiences in Liberia. Washington notes the country's struggles and the shortage of physicians. He also comments on the role of the United States in Liberian affairs.

Washington's belief that emancipation alone would not aid the plight of freed blacks prompted him to resettle in Liberia in 1853, where he remained until his death in 1875.

Augustus Washington, "Liberia as It Is, 1854," *Liberian Dreams: Back-to-Africa Narratives from the 1850s,* edited by Wilson Jeremiah Moses. University Park: Pennsylvania State University Press, 1998.

Monrovia, June 27, 1854

I n a residence of six months in Liberia, I have met with nothing so "passing strange" as the fact that no one has made known to the American public the sufferings of Southern emigrants after their arrival here, the paucity of physicians, and in some instances their shameful neglect of duty. I am aware that this cannot be done without incurring the censure of some persons in this country who at present occupy high official stations, who have become influential and comparatively wealthy by conniving at these faults, and who for this have the full confidence of the Agents of the American Colonization Society. I know too that for my presumption in exposing these wrongs as the only means of reform, I must fall under the displeasure of these gentlemen and perhaps of some few illiberal members of the Society. But I have a strong consolation in knowing that here I have the hearts and sympathies of the common people with me—the masses who are poor, whose letters of complaint have been [intercepted] and kept from the public, and whose wrongs have never been redressed.

If the Promise Were Fulfilled

There are thousands of colonizationists in the States, North and South, who contribute their money to the cause with the best and most benevolent motives—men who honestly wish to elevate, christianize and bless Africa, and make free and happy her unfortunate descendants—men who have hearts in the right place and always sympathize with crushed humanity, whether in Greece, Turkey, Hungary, or Africa, and have no desire to send men to these unhappy shores, only sicken and die for want of suitable food and medical attendance, while, if the promise of the Society were truthfully filled, instead of thirty, forty, fifty, and sixty, not more than six per cent of the emigrants would die. These gentlemen have a right to know the facts of the case. Senator Russell declares to me that he has written four times to the agents on the very subject, and has received no satisfaction. A few other citizens have written and some emigrants have done so; but who has ever met with their complaints in any public paper, while some execrable cowards, who complain most of the *Society* and everything American talk one thing here and another thing to the States to please the people, have their letters published in all the papers. Not only public, but even private letters of such persons as President Roberts, Judge Benson, and their adherents, are all given to the

public and then a brood of young aspirants for office and colonization patronage follow in the wake of their elder brethren. Even
many new comers will write fine things of this country which they
never have seen, and of which they have only read.

> They talk of the beauties which they never saw
> And fancy raptures they will never know.

The Country Struggles

"I would rather be right than President." I shall maintain the cause
of God and humanity, and the poor emigrant and native regardless
of consequences. I know that by a different course, I could soon
grow rich by the suffering and death of those poor people. For, in
nearly every town and county, there is a one-man power, for that
county; a man may hold all the offices of government and besides
be lawyer, merchant, judge, and agent for the Society, and, if he
chooses, it is not difficult to turn the money and offices of these
people into his own coffers. But if I have health and the same
amount of brains, I can become wealthy if that be a virtue without
aid from the Colonization Society, this feeble Government, or the
men who see their daguerreotypes in the group I have pictured. For
every mouthful of beer we get, we are equally dependent on the
natives. When they choose to "kick up a row" (which often hap-
pens) and make war among themselves, we can get no meat, sometimes for months. We have no regular market; but when a beef is
occasionally brought to market, I have seen six different hands
pulling at two pounds of beef, while the butcher was carving it up,
and, thus quarreling, and playing a regular "grab game" for a little
meat, and seldom is there anything like a supply. And why is this?
Because scarcely any of the people in this city work, but nearly all
sit down and depend on living by trade with the natives and thus,
while a few with capital grow rich, most of them live only from
hand to mouth. Since all alike depend on the natives for their living, why need anyone fear to do right for the value of the patronage of the Society, or the smiles of a few in transient power? Their
policy with the natives has been an unwise one. The latter are not
found in our schools, and seldom in our churches. One teacher tells
me he has about sixty scholars, but not one native. While they give
no encouragement to education among them, fearing they will get
power some day, they sell them any quantity of muskets with
which to blow out our brains; when a wiser policy would be to

make it a penal offense to sell them muskets and powder, but educate them, regard them as men, and incorporate them in community. There is but little regard for poor emigrants, yet I value them most because they are the working men, the bone and sinew of the community. They are the only men that would cultivate the soil and become the producers, and without such the country will only struggle on as now, in poverty, till it meets with some reverse, and falls as a colony into the hands of some European power. Think of the fact. We only live on the seaboard, or a few miles up the rivers. We have put a single road five miles up the rivers. We have not a single road five miles into the interior. All the region behind us is land unknown. The hundreds of tribes in our rear have only to unite and they can at any time drive us into the ocean. And yet, to hear the windy speeches of our orators, one might suppose that all Africa had been conquered, and our lone star banner unfurled in every country from the Cape of Good Hope to the Mediterranean, from Guardafui to Cape Verde.

A Dark Unwritten Chapter

When I published in *The Tribune* in 1851 my views in favor of African colonization, I could not believe that the opponents of the scheme had uttered so much truth. In that communication the only thing I have since found to regret was my advocacy of the proposed line of steamers to this coast, and this regret is only for the reason that there is as yet no suitable preparation made for emigrants as to comfortable houses, and proper medical attendance by the American Colonization Society nor the United States Government. Still I have charity enough to believe that if the former and latter knew these things as they are, if the Society was not able, the Government itself, for humanity's sake, would do something to aid them. Many of us new comers clapped our hands with joy that the *Shirley*, which has just arrived, brought no emigrants; but our joy was soon turned to sorrow when we learned that the *Sophia Walker* would soon arrive with a large number from Baltimore. Unfortunate wretches! What will they do in the midst of these driving rains packed down in these leaky huts in which gentlemen in the States would not keep their horses and favorite dogs. The state of things here, years ago, in regard to the treatment and suffering of emigrants was heart-rending and almost incredible, and yet no one who had not the means and opportunity to leave the country dared report them. They have greatly changed now for the better, and yet there is a dark chapter that never has been written. All the letters from Liberia, published in papers in the States give too high a coloring to everything pertaining to the country. It is no Paradise, no Elysium, no Eldorado. It is the last refuge of the oppressed colored man, and a country that could as easily have been subjected by the whites, if they had no other, and were thus compelled to make the same sacrifice of thousands of lives. We northern emigrants by the *Isla de Cuba* have fared well enough and thus for ourselves have no very special public complaint. Our sufferings are nothing in comparison. Having some means of our own, we have all resided at the Cape in Monrovia, where we could more easily obtain medical attendance, comfortable houses, and tolerably good food. Besides we have all been within the reach of the kindness of the wealthy class of citizens who have often favored us in sickness by their kind offices, and with suitable and nourishing regimen which our money could not buy. The *Banshee* with two hundred and seventy three emigrants arrived the same day we did, and the agent Mr. Dennis, according to instructions from Washington sent about two hundred of them up the St. Paul's River, crowding as many as possible into the United States Receptacle, and scattering the rest along the banks of the river, into such houses as could be procured. And these are small huts—generally one story high, with only a single room, from ten to twelve feet square, and into which a whole family, from five to twelve or fifteen are placed. Many of these huts are built of twigs interwoven; and plastered outside with common mud. The thatched roofs let down any quantity of water on their beds and often they are compelled to change their positions constantly, and hold their umbrellas to escape being saturated with rain.

The Emigrant's Plight

But what are the facts in regard to this U.S. Receptacle? It is an old, shabby, rickety building, originally designed for the *Pons* captives, and since used by the Colonization Society for the reception and six months residence of emigrants. It is only one story high, with a garret, and is built of brick—It contains twelve pens below and four garret apartments. These rooms (if they deserve such a name) are about six feet by nine, having one small window without glass, which must be closed during the rains and at night, thus making a suitable dungeon for a murderer. Within these rooms, I have seen nothing but an excuse for a bedstead made out of rough saplings lashed together with bark or rope, and stuck up against one side of each stall, about four feet from the floor. I first visited this place, and saw these stalls, about three weeks after my arrival in this country and remarked to my friends, that if I had to stay in one of them, I should surely expect to die. I saw nothing else in these except what the emigrants had brought, and upon this baggage many of them had to make their seats. Some of these stalls contained each whole families of six to ten and fourteen. Dr. Jacob M. Moore, who was employed by the agent here to attend them for the six months, declared to me that they had no place to keep their provisions except under their beds, and there, at any time, you would find their rations of salt beef, salt pork, rotten fish, &c, with all other indescribable necessaries. Besides this there are always some sick persons in bed. *This fever is no humbug.* It is a stern reality, and of a family of six, after two months they never will find three successive days that all of them are well, short of six or nine months. Thus I maintain that the best house in town, and the best of medical skill, and the best of fresh food are nothing too good for an emigrant if he can afford it, while passing through the raw ordeal of acclimation. But such is the development of hope in the Afric American (the Fowlers will sustain me) that whatever may be the suffering and misery he endures, as soon as he escapes them, he forgets the past, and descants with rapture on the future. Who does not know how miserable, servile and degraded is the condition of the free colored people in the States?—and yet Messrs. Pennington, Frederick Douglass & Co. preach to these people the certainty of elevation and social and political equality in America, while the million, educated free from their prejudices, could not come to such a conclusion in their wildest dreams of philanthropy. The former would accomplish much more good for our race, if they would come over and help us correct the abuses and oppression here, and make this country what it might be, than by staying there and wasting their energies in exhausting efforts, which always avail nothing. I have just taken the pains to measure a hut one story high, with one room and garret, twelve by sixteen feet into which seventeen of the emigrants of the *Banshee* were placed, and in which they remained nearly two months till the fever broke out, when they were separated, leaving ten in the hut. Another hut close by has four persons in one room, twelve by fourteen feet. This is the way they live. We think they have in Mr. H. W. Dennis, an honest, upright faithful and attentive agent; but there are no better houses to be obtained for small rent, and he is not furnished with any money by the Society, but is compelled to trade, and twist many ways to meet the cash payments for the rent, nursing and washing, &c., of the emigrants or compel the Society's creditors to take trade goods and provisions when they do not want them. He has the confidence of this community, and we all think he will do right, and give satisfaction to the emigrants to the full extent of the power and means conferred upon him by the Society. He is the man, perhaps the only man here that does or ever did give his whole attention to this business exclusively. The emigrants by the *Isla de Cuba* have petitioned to the Directors of the New York State Society to send their friends in future to Mr. Dennis; but it seems to me unfair unless they also give him an additional small salary. Such a man, if he were white, possessing the same qualifications, would receive a salary of twelve or fifteen hundred dollars, while now he receives only six or seven hundred. Any man like him can make four times this amount by trade; and I shall be sorry for the poor emigrants if they lose him.

Educated and Skillful Physicians Needed

No class of men are more needed in this country than thoroughly educated and skillful physicians. I never have heard of a country in which life is so cheap. But here again is one man power. The Society employ regularly but one physician—Dr. Roberts—whose estimate of poor emigrants is very small. While he will visit some few of the reputed wealthy families of Northern emigrants three times a day uncalled, the majority of the rest can get no attention; and the poor Southern emigrants declare to me that they send, and send, and send again, and he will not see them himself once in two or three weeks, and sometimes in two or three months, but he will send them a boy or heathen native with calomel, oil, and pills, and will doctor them in this way, and if these do not cure, they must die. One poor family, and the single men have been treated in this way. People here generally build houses by piece-meal, occupying some years in completion. The Doctor's time has been absorbed in building his house this year, and I think some years before. Now, in these circumstances the Society should have employed some one to assist him in medical practice. This neglect of duty is partly owing to the want of competition and an independent supervision by some agent or commissioner who is too honest and brave to be influenced in favor of wrong by kind treatment, good wine, or splendid dinners. I have heard this same complaint twice, in whispers in the States, and hundreds of times here. But poor men, as the mass of emigrants are, they dare not make any complaint public against the Society or its agents or against the Government functionaries of this Republic, fearing the loss of daily bread, if not their lives. Thus glaring wrongs have existed here for a long time which the rich grow fat on, and the poor, for their lives dare not meddle with—They tell us we must take men as they are—we must not disturb their passions—we must not arouse their prejudices. To take men as they are in any such sense, is to leave them worse, than you find them; an angel's spear must be had, whose touch will bring the toad to a proper shape, though it start up a devil. I would rather live a serf under the Czar of Russia, than in a country where I must employ a physician in whose carefulness, responsibility, and skill I have no confidence. The want of competition keeps some men always at the point from which they started, and the dependence of the community renders them petty kings. The truth is when emigrants come here by hundreds at a time, Dr. Roberts has more than he can properly attend to, even with the occasional assistance of Dr. J.M. Moore. But this is no reason that he should do less than his duty. In justice to Dr. Roberts, I may here say, that I have no fault to find with him except in his medical practice as the Society's physician. In my intercourse with him as a citizen, I find him kind, generous, and affable as most persons I meet with. Besides, he is yet a young man, and, if he would study and carefully practice, is capable of rising to the head and leading the van, of the medical fraternity in this country. I have no personal quarrel with nor enmity against the Doctor. But individuals have complained of this and other wrongs to the agents of the American Colonization Society in vain. As a last resort, I write this publicly in behalf of many hungry orphan children, and wretched widows, made desolate by the loss of their husbands who have died for want of food or medical attendance, in a strange and foreign land. I do not wish the Society to throw him overboard, but simply demand a greater degree of attention to poor emigrants—a higher grade of skill and efficiency in himself, and then pay him a better salary. Because this is a dear country in which to live comfortably, and the man who gives his whole attention to any one department of business deserves to be well paid. . . .

Easier in America

I will not harrow up your minds by any accounts of fearful mortality caused by the want of medical attention and the comforts of life among poor emigrants. Suffice it say that of two hundred of the emigrants of the *Banshee* (which arrived at the time we did) sent up the St. Paul's river, one third have died, and our agents, citizens, and physicians are all in controversy about it, in two party papers, published in this city, called the *Herald* and *Sentinel*. If any colonization papers doubt my statements, let them only dare publish the letters from these papers. It will all come out. Let them only state one fact and comment in future. I have spent one whole day investigating the case of the *Morgan Dix*, which sailed from Baltimore Nov. 1, 1851 and arrived at Bassa with one hundred and fifty one, all well. . . . They were then supplied with means—with a saw mill and agricultural implements.—But where are they now? Echo answers, where? Could the grave disgorge those gun boxes into which their corpses were buried, it would disclose a horrid tale of the neglect of the physician, agent, or Society—or exhibit the murderous work of sending fresh emigrants to people new districts of country that resemble no place so much as Golgotha. Read and understand that of *these one hundred and fifty one emigrants there are but nine survivors.* Others maintain there are fourteen. Grant that there are fourteen survivors. I challenge the Colonization Society and their agents here and in America to prove that there are more. And all this is the result of sending men to the most unhealthy part of this country, and packing them into old, rickety thatched houses, in which the emigrants tell me they had to hold umbrellas to keep them from the pelting rain. Besides these have but one physician for Bassa and Sinoe, which I think are one hundred and fifty miles apart, and I have too much evidence not to believe that some of the emigrants actually starve and die for want of food and medical care.—But let me speak softly. I well nigh forget that I must buy my goods and provisions in New York, Boston, and Baltimore for my store, and after talking so loudly, I may be troubled to find an agent to discount my drafts, and forward goods in colonization vessels. Besides, I may be persecuted by a pack of hungry pork-eaters in Liberia. With the physicians I have done at present. From Dr. Roberts and his particular friends I may expect resentment. But if I can only save from the grave a few poor Southern emigrants and make better the chances of long life to my friends from the North, I am willing the doctor shall pay me for my boldness in any kind of coin he pleases. Injustice to the Society I may say that this case of the *Morgan Dix* is an extraordinary one. The emigrants of the *Isla de Cuba*, in which I came having settled at this place, have lost only three of their number, and seem to be doing well; and the *Banshee*, as I have said, which arrived the same day, lost of her two hundred—sent only fifteen miles up the river—one third. Some of my friends write me and inquire how I like the country. I may say, on the whole, first rate, and if I did not, I could return to the States to morrow, $1,000 better off than when I came here six or seven months ago. I have had three pokers in the fire and God has prospered me with all, although I have been sick at times, as much as three months; wife sick constantly: children well now: I invite my friends to come to Liberia, but take care to have some little means to start with. You can earn it in America easier than in Africa— Where one succeeds with nothing, twenty suffer and die, leaving no mark of their existence.

Prometheus Unbound's Timeless Themes

by Desmond King-Hele

English poet Percy Bysshe Shelley's *Prometheus Unbound: A Lyrical Drama in Four Acts*, published in the summer of 1820, represents the spirit of the romantic movement. Although the seeds of romanticism are in the late eighteenth century, the movement flourished in the early and middle nineteenth century. Romanticism, which emerged in response to the reason-centered Enlightenment movement of the eighteenth century, emphasized emotion, love of nature, heroism, adventure, and imagination. The "Romantics," as intellectuals and artists who subscribed to the movement are called, believed poetry to be the highest form of literary expression and a direct reflection of the soul.

As a romantic poet, Shelley sought to reform the world through his literary works. *Prometheus Unbound*, based on Greek mythology, symbolizes humankind's revolt against the laws and customs that oppress the freedom for which human nature compels us to long.

In the following selection, Desmond King-Hele examines the significance of *Prometheus Unbound* to the literary world. He explains the merits of the complex poem as well as Shelley's purpose in re-creating the Greek myth. King-Hele notes that the poem conveys the notion that man can improve his status and that the world can be a happier place.

A physicist by trade, Desmond King-Hele is fellow of the Royal Society and the author of over fifteen books.

Desmond King-Hele, *Shelley: The Man and the Poet*. New York: Thomas Yoseloff, 1960.

*P*rometheus Unbound, a 'lyrical drama in four acts', is the greatest, though not the most perfect, of Shelley's poems, difficult to grasp in all its detail, yet clear enough in its broad aims. We are given a preview of Man's escape from the restraints now stifling him, and a forecast of the principles which he will have accepted before he attains the maximum of happiness and freedom open to him. Prometheus represents the mind of Man, and his liberation is symbolic of Man's.

A "New" Myth

The writing of *Prometheus Unbound* was done in three short spells. Act I was written in September and October 1818 at Este, near Venice; Acts II and III in March and April 1819 at Rome among the ruins of the Baths of Caracalla, under a 'bright blue sky'; and Act IV in November and December 1819 at Florence. The subject had been in Shelley's mind for over a year before he began to write—an unusually long incubation period for him—and he had considered Tasso and Job, as well as Prometheus, for his hero.

One of his reasons for picking the legend of Prometheus was the disagreement between the classical versions of it, which left him free to choose between them. According to ancient [Greek poet] Hesiod, Prometheus brought calamity on mankind when he angered the gods by stealing fire from heaven, and the innocent golden age came to an end. Shelley accepted this view in 1813 when, as a vegetarian, he eyed with distaste the inventor of cooking. But he never took kindly to the idea of a primaeval golden age, and by 1819 he preferred Aeschylus's version of the legend, as implied in the *Prometheus Bound*. There Prometheus appears as Man's benefactor, who brought fire, number, writing, medicine and the arts as gifts from heaven to the hitherto ignorant, beast-like mortals. This impudence infuriated Zeus, chief of the gods and no friend to men. So Zeus had him chained to a rock in the Caucasus. There Prometheus remains at the end of Aeschylus's play, nursing a secret known to him alone: that if Zeus should marry Thetis, he would beget a son more powerful than himself— a prophecy Zeus would have found horribly plausible, since he had ousted his own father Cronos. Unless he reveals this secret, Prometheus is doomed to remain shackled in the icy mountains for thirty thousand years, his entrails being devoured daily by an eagle (or, in some versions, a vulture). The *Prometheus Bound* was the second part of a trilogy, and Aeschylus completed the story in the third part, *Prometheus Unbound*, now lost, where Prometheus was reconciled with Zeus.

Shelley creates a new myth from the skeleton of the old. In his version Prometheus remains in torment until the time is ripe for Demogorgon, the destined son of Zeus and Thetis, to overthrow his father. After the downfall of Jupiter (Shelley uses the Roman names for Zeus and the other gods), Prometheus is formally unbound by Hercules. Shelley chose a story with familiar names in it so that his readers might feel at home among the *dramatis personae* and pass with less effort in identification to the powers they represent—probably a better plan than bringing on personifications like Faith and Evil, or reviving obscure names, as [poet William] Blake too often did. The drama thus unfolds on two levels: ostensibly it records a reshuffling of power among the Olympians; at the deeper level each character represents some trait in Man, preferably a trait associated with that character in legend. Thus the fact that Prometheus suffers avoidable pain implies that Man is cruelly restricted by unnecessary chains; while Jupiter's fall is more impressive because, to minds conditioned by Greek myth, his name spells irresistible power. . . .

Man Can Improve His Status

To gather the threads again after so many pages of detail it may be as well to recapitulate the myth embodied in *Prometheus Unbound*. Jupiter has chained Prometheus because he helped men to better themselves and would not yield up his secret—that the child of Jupiter and Thetis would overthrow his father. Prometheus defies the Furies sent to torture him, and shows he is wise, kindly and free from rancour. He thinks of Asia, his long-lost bride. She responds by visiting Demogorgon, the destined child of Jupiter, in his lair outside the physical world. Very soon after, Demogorgon ascends to Heaven, deposes Jupiter and retires to obscurity. Prometheus is unbound by Hercules and united to Asia.

This enigmatic sequence of events must be interpreted as myth rather than allegory. A detailed translation of the events into another medium, as in allegory, is not to be expected. It is rather the broad outlines which are of importance, some of the details being irrelevant. For example, the fact that Demogorgon is said to be Jupiter's son is not significant: it is merely a detail taken over from the Greek legend. The need to preselect the vital points makes it harder to interpret the myth. Shelley himself thought only five or six people would understand the poem, and Mary warns us in her Note [wife Mary Shelley penned an explanatory note about the poem] that 'it requires a mind as subtle and penetrating as his own to understand the mystic meanings scattered throughout the poem. They elude the ordinary reader by their abstraction and delicacy of distinction, but they are far from vague.' These warnings need not deter us unduly, for now that so many scholars have exercised their wits on the poem most of the subtleties Mary mentions have been exposed, though it is only fair to add that each new commentator seems to find more.

There is little doubt that Shelley's chief aim is to forecast that Man can greatly improve his status, becoming almost unrecognizably happier and wiser, if, and only if, he first develops and encourages—genuinely, not with mere lip-service—the Christian virtues of universal love and forgiveness. When Prometheus, Man's representative, shows he has these qualities, Jupiter, the reactionary power, the 'everlasting No', will topple from his throne. Then Prometheus will wed Asia; so Man will combine wisdom, tolerance and endurance with love and creative power, and live in harmony with Nature.

Though it is generally agreed that this was Shelley's aim, several variants have been suggested, and the most important of them is the political interpretation. Shelley certainly implies that political systems change when Jupiter falls (though he always believed reform would be gradual, and Jupiter's fall is sudden in the poem only because of the need for a recognizable dramatic catastrophe). According to the political interpretation, Jupiter's fall means reform's triumph, Prometheus represents the enlightened thinkers of Shelley's day, Mercury the supine drudges in the pay of the governing classes (Jupiter), and the Furies the sycophants who grow fat on the spoils of their master and let off steam by persecuting reformers. These identifications are not without a grain of truth, but since Asia and Demogorgon are difficult to fit in, the political variant is at best an illuminating side-issue. . . .

A Happier World

In *Prometheus Unbound* Shelley succeeds in working his moral, political and philosophical ideals into a well-knit poetic theme. He also successfully fuses the two sides of his nature, the rational and the emotional, which had inspired *Queen Mab* and *Alastor* respectively. *Prometheus Unbound* is free from the touches of hysteria, the extremism, the inconsistencies and the bias which marred his previous long poems, and although some faults remain, Shelley is not wholly to blame for them. The poem could be clearer, for example, but the obscurity is not wilful: it is the result of a struggle to communicate ideas which are beyond the resources of language. And, as a second example, the poem is rather feeble as a drama, but not because Shelley digresses: structurally the poem is one of his best, and he never strays far from the theme in Acts I–III. Then, in the detached Act IV, the events of Acts I–III are celebrated chorally. Though Act IV adds nothing to the plot, no one would wish to see it omitted, because it is unique in English poetry for its intimate blend of exact science and dazzling verse, its sustained animation and exultation, and its pervading philosophy of unity in Nature. It is creative myth of a high order, a reminder that Shelley was 'the most spontaneous of myth-makers and the most scientifically-minded poet of the age'.

It would be churlish to find fault with the spirit which animates the poem. Shelley looks forward to a happier world based on Christian charity between men: cynics may scoff, but can they offer anything better?

Prometheus Unbound will not make its fullest appeal until the world is more settled. But even in this troubled century it has had its champions. In the words of Sir Maurice Bowra, 'His triumph is that . . . through the enchantment which his poetry sets on us we are able to explore regions of which he is the discoverer and almost the only denizen, and to know in his company the delights of a condition in which the old quarrel of poetry and philosophy is healed and the pallid abstractions of analytical thought take on the glow and the glory of visible things'. *Prometheus Unbound* was 'for many years a sort of gospel' to Gilbert Murray, who knew nearly all of it by heart. W.B. Yeats, on re-reading it, remarked that 'it seems to me to have an even more certain place than I had thought among the sacred books of the world'. And Sir Herbert Read has called it 'the greatest expression ever given to humanity's desire for intellectual light and spiritual liberty'.

13

Percy Bysshe Shelley Publishes
Prometheus Unbound: Summer 1820

My Passion Is to Reform the World

by Percy Bysshe Shelley

Percy Bysshe Shelley (1792–1822) is one of the most famous poets of the romantic era. His works reveal themes of brooding despair, antiauthoritarianism, a search for freedom, a belief in ideal love, and the powers of poetry. Shelley pursued controversial issues (he was expelled from school for promoting atheism) even if it rendered him unpopular.

Shelley's masterpiece *Prometheus Unbound: A Lyrical Drama in Four Acts*, was published in the summer of 1820. The poetic play expresses romantic themes through Greek mythology. It was influenced by *Prometheus Bound* by the ancient Greek playwright Aeschylus. According to mythology, Prometheus (the name means "forethought") was a Titan (giant) who was punished for stealing fire from the gods and giving it to humanity. He is a character associated with rebellion and isolation. Shelley depicted Prometheus as a symbol of man's mind or soul exploring its greatest potential and a figure epitomizing romantic ideals.

The following is Shelley's preface to *Prometheus Unbound*. In it, he not only explains the subject and purpose of the work but also reveals his influences and the reasons behind his choices of imagery. Shelley also expresses his desire to reform the world through poetry and his conviction that poetry is essential for understanding and achieving moral excellence.

Percy Bysshe Shelley remains an influential and controversial figure in the study of romantic poetry. He died at age twenty-nine as a result of a drowning accident in the Mediterranean Sea.

Percy Bysshe Shelley, "Prometheus Unbound: A Lyrical Drama in Four Acts," www.english.upenn.edu.

The Greek tragic writers, in selecting as their subject any portion of their national history or mythology, employed in their treatment of it a certain arbitrary discretion. They by no means conceived themselves bound to adhere to the common interpretation or to imitate in story as in title their rivals and predecessors. Such a system would have amounted to a resignation of those claims to preference over their competitors which incited the composition. The Agamemnonian story was exhibited on the Athenian theatre with as many variations as dramas.

Influence and Imagery

I have presumed to employ a similar license. The Prometheus Unbound of Æschylus supposed the reconciliation of Jupiter with his victim as the price of the disclosure of the danger threatened to his empire by the consummation of his marriage with Thetis. Thetis, according to this view of the subject, was given in marriage to Peleus, and Prometheus, by the permission of Jupiter, delivered from his captivity by Hercules. Had I framed my story on this model, I should have done no more than have attempted to restore the lost drama of Æschylus; an ambition which, if my preference to this mode of treating the subject had incited me to cherish, the recollection of the high comparison such an attempt would challenge might well abate. But, in truth, I was averse from a catastrophe so feeble as that of reconciling the Champion with the Oppressor of mankind. The moral interest of the fable, which is so powerfully sustained by the sufferings and endurance of Prometheus, would be annihilated if we could conceive of him as unsaying his high language and quailing before his successful and perfidious adversary. The only imaginary being, resembling in any degree Prometheus, is Satan; and Prometheus is, in my judgment, a more poetical character than Satan, because, in addition to courage, and majesty, and firm and patient opposition to omnipotent force, he is susceptible of being described as exempt from the taints of ambition, envy, revenge, and a desire for personal aggrandizement, which, in the hero of Paradise Lost, interfere with the interest. The character of Satan engenders in the mind a pernicious casuistry which leads us to weigh his faults with his wrongs, and to excuse the former because the latter exceed all measure. In the minds of those who consider that magnificent fiction with a religious feeling it engenders something worse. But Prometheus is, as it were, the type of the highest perfection of moral and intellectual nature impelled by the purest and the truest motives to the best and noblest ends.

This Poem was chiefly written upon the mountainous ruins of the Baths of Caracalla, among the flowery glades and thickets of odoriferous blossoming trees, which are extended in ever winding labyrinths upon its immense platforms and dizzy arches suspended in the air. The bright blue sky of Rome, and the effect of the vigorous awakening spring in that divinest climate, and the new life with which it drenches the spirits even to intoxication, were the inspiration of this drama.

The imagery which I have employed will be found, in many instances, to have been drawn from the operations of the human mind, or from those external actions by which they are expressed. This is unusual in modern poetry, although Dante and Shakespeare are full of instances of the same kind; Dante indeed more than any other poet, and with greater success. But the Greek poets, as writers to whom no resource of awakening the sympathy of their contemporaries was unknown, were in the habitual use of this power; and it is the study of their works (since a higher merit would probably be denied me) to which I am willing that my readers should impute this singularity.

One word is due in candor to the degree in which the study of contemporary writings may have tinged my composition, for such has been a topic of censure with regard to poems far more popular, and indeed more deservedly popular, than mine. It is impossible that any one, who inhabits the same age with such writers as those who stand in the foremost ranks of our own, can conscientiously assure himself that his language and tone of thought may not have been modified by the study of the productions of those extraordinary intellects. It is true that, not the spirit of their genius, but the forms in which it has manifested itself, are due less to the peculiarities of their own minds than to the peculiarity of the moral and intellectual condition of the minds among which they have been produced. Thus a number of writers possess the form, whilst they want the spirit of those whom, it is alleged, they imitate; because the former is the endowment of the age in which they live, and the latter must be the uncommunicated lightning of their own mind.

A Passion for Reforming the World

The peculiar style of intense and comprehensive imagery which distinguishes the modern literature of England has not been, as a general power, the product of the imitation of any particular writer. The mass of capabilities remains at every period materially the same; the circumstances which awaken it to action perpetually change. If England were divided into forty republics, each equal in population and extent to Athens, there is no reason to suppose but that, under institutions not more perfect than those of Athens, each would produce philosophers and poets equal to those who (if we except Shakespeare) have never been surpassed. We owe the great writers of the golden age of our literature to that fervid awakening of the public mind which shook to dust the oldest and most oppressive form of the Christian religion. We owe [John] Milton to the progress and development of the same spirit: the sacred Milton was, let it ever be remembered, a republican and a bold inquirer into morals and religion. The great writers of our own age are, we have reason to suppose, the companions and forerunners of some unimagined change in our social condition or the opinions which cement it. The cloud of mind is discharging its collected lightning, and the equilibrium between institutions and opinions is now restoring or is about to be restored.

As to imitation, poetry is a mimetic art. It creates, but it creates by combination and representation. Poetical abstractions are beautiful and new, not because the portions of which they are composed had no previous existence in the mind of man or in Nature, but because the whole produced by their combination has some intelligible and beautiful analogy with those sources of emotion and thought and with the contemporary condition of them. One great poet is a masterpiece of Nature which another not only ought to study but must study. He might as wisely and as easily determine that his mind should no longer be the mirror of all that is lovely in the visible universe as exclude from his contemplation the beautiful which exists in the writings of a great contemporary. The pretence of doing it would be a presumption in any but the greatest; the effect, even in him, would be strained, unnatural and ineffectual. A poet is the combined product of such internal powers as modify the nature of others, and of such external influences as excite and sustain these powers; he is not one, but both. Every man's mind is, in this respect, modified by all the objects of Nature and art; by every word and every suggestion which he ever admitted to act upon his consciousness; it is the mirror upon which all forms are reflected and in which they compose one form. Poets, not otherwise than philosophers, painters, sculptors and musicians, are, in one sense, the creators, and, in another, the creations, of their age. From this subjection the loftiest do not escape. There is a similarity between Homer and Hesiod, between Æschylus and Euripides, between Virgil and Horace, between Dante and Petrarch, between Shakespeare and [John] Fletcher, between [John] Dryden and [Alexander] Pope; each has a generic resemblance under which their specific distinctions are arranged. If this similarity be the result of imitation, I am willing to confess that I have imitated.

Let this opportunity be conceded to me of acknowledging that I have what a Scotch philosopher characteristically terms a 'passion for reforming the world:' what passion incited him to write and publish his book he omits to explain. For my part I had rather be damned with Plato and Lord Bacon than go to Heaven with [William] Paley and [Thomas] Malthus. But it is a mistake to suppose that I dedicate my poetical compositions solely to the direct enforcement of reform, or that I consider them in any degree as containing a reasoned system on the theory of human life. Didactic poetry is my abhorrence; nothing can be equally well expressed in prose that is not tedious and supererogatory in verse. My purpose has hitherto been simply to familiarize the highly refined imagination of the more select classes of poetical readers with beautiful idealisms of moral excellence; aware that, until the mind can love, and admire, and trust, and hope, and endure, reasoned principles of moral conduct are seeds cast upon the highway of life which the unconscious passenger tramples into dust, although they would bear the harvest of his happiness. Should I live to accomplish what I purpose, that is, produce a systematical history of what appear to me to be the genuine elements of human society, let not the advocates of injustice and superstition flatter themselves that I should take Æschylus rather than Plato as my model.

The having spoken of myself with unaffected freedom will need little apology with the candid; and let the uncandid consider that they injure me less than their own hearts and minds by misrepresentation. Whatever talents a person may possess to amuse and instruct others, be they ever so inconsiderable, he is yet bound to exert them: if his attempt be ineffectual, let the punishment of an unaccomplished purpose have been sufficient; let none trouble themselves to heap the dust of oblivion upon his efforts; the pile they raise will betray his grave which might otherwise have been unknown.

CHRONOLOGY

1800
Thomas Jefferson is elected president of the United States.

1801
January 1: The union of Great Britain and Ireland takes effect.

1802
Madame Marie Tussaud opens her wax museum in London. The museum remains in operation to the present day.

1803
April 30: The Louisiana Purchase treaty is signed. France sells territory to the United States that nearly doubles the size of the nation.

1804
May 14: Meriwether Lewis and William Clark begin a U.S. government–sponsored, transcontinental exploration.
December 2: Napoléon crowns himself emperor of France.

1805
April 7: In Vienna, Beethoven's Third Symphony, the *Eroica*, is performed publicly for the first time.
October 21: The British have a lopsided victory over Napoléon in a naval battle at Trafalgar; British admiral Horatio Nelson is killed by a sharpshooter.

1806
Napoléon dissolves the centuries-old German confederation called the Holy Roman Empire.
September 23: Lewis and Clark return from their expedition.

1807
August 14: The first steamboat trip is made from New York City to Albany.

1808
Johann Wolfgang Goethe publishes part one of *Faust*.

1809
January 19: Edgar Allan Poe is born.

1810
May 25: Argentina revolts from Spanish colonial rule, spawning a series of revolutions throughout Latin America.

1812
Grimms' Fairy Tales is published.
February/March: The Luddite riots, in which skilled craftsmen destroy machines as a protest against industrial mechanization, take place in England.
June 18: The War of 1812 between the United States and Great Britain begins.

1814
April: Napoléon is defeated following a retreat from Russia that led to the War of Liberation of Europe (1813–1814).
Louis XVIII of the Bourbon dynasty, the family that ruled prior to Napoléon's reign, becomes king of France.
October 1: The Congress of Vienna convenes.

1815
February 17: The War of 1812 ends.
June 9: The Congress of Vienna ends.
June 18: British commander Wellington defeats Napoléon at the Battle of Waterloo, which is the emperor's final military campaign.

1816
The American Colonization Society, which aims to help free blacks immigrate to Africa, is founded.

1817

The Wartburg Festival takes places in Germany. Five hundred students from twelve universities burn "reactionary" books and celebrate German nationalism.

1818

The Webster-Ashburton Treaty is signed, declaring the forty-ninth parallel to be the U.S-Canadian border.
Chile, freed the previous year by José de San Martín's forces, declares independence from Spain.

1819

Hans C. Oersted discovers electromagnetism. Simon Bolívar's forces free Colombia from Spanish rule. The United States purchases Florida from Spain.

1820

Percy Bysshe Shelley's *Prometheus Unbound* is published.
February 6: Free blacks sail from New York to Africa as part of a colonization movement.
March: The Missouri Compromise is passed in the United States. Maine enters the Union as a free state, and Missouri enters as a slave state.

FOR FURTHER RESEARCH

Books

John Logan Allen, *Passage Through the Garden: Lewis and Clark and the Image of the American Northwest.* Urbana: University of Illinois Press, 1975.

Robert Asprey, *The Rise of Napoleon Bonaparte.* New York: Basic Books, 2001.

Ludwig van Beethoven, *Beethoven's Letters (1790–1826) from the Collection of Ludwig Nohl.* Trans. Lady Wallace. Boston: Longwood, 1978.

Carl Benn, *The War of 1812.* New York: Routledge, 2003.

Louis Antoine Fauvelet de Bourrienne, *Memoirs of Napoleon Bonaparte.* New York: Scribner, 1889.

Helmut Brackert and Volkman Sander, eds., *Jakob and Wilhelm Grimm and Others: German Fairy Tales.* New York: Continuum, 1985.

Claude A. Clegg III, *The Price of Liberty: African Americans and the Making of Liberia.* Chapel Hill: University of North Carolina Press, 2004.

Ludwig Dehio, *The Precarious Balance.* New York: Alfred A. Knopf, 1962.

Michael Duffy, *The Younger Pitt.* New York: Longman, 2000.

Marilyn Gaull, *English Romanticism: The Human Context.* New York: Norton, 1988.

Leo Gershoy, *The French Revolution and Napoleon.* New York: Appleton-Century-Crofts, 1933.

Jakob and Wilhelm Grimm, *Household Stories Collected by the Brothers Grimm.* London: Routledge, 1901.

A.D. Harvey, *Britain in the Early Nineteenth Century.* New York: St. Martin's Press, 1978.

Donald R. Hickey, *The War of 1812: A Short History.* Urbana: University of Illinois Press, 1995.

Christa Kamenetsky, *The Brothers Grimm and Their Critics: Folktales and the Quest for Meaning.* Athens: Ohio University Press, 1992.

Peter J. Kastor, *Nation's Crucible: The Louisiana Purchase and the Creation of America.* New Haven, CT: Yale University Press, 2004.

Charles W. Kegley Jr. and Gregory A. Raymond, *From War to Peace: Fateful Decisions in International Politics.* Boston: Bedford/St. Martin's, 2002.

Desmond King-Hele, *Shelley: The Man and the Poet.* New York: Thomas Yoseloff, 1960.

Henry Kissinger, *A World Restored: Metternich, Castlereagh, and the Problems of Peace.* Boston: Houghton Mifflin, 1973.

Jon Kukla, *So Immense: The Louisiana Purchase and the Destiny of America.* New York: Alfred A. Knopf, 2003.

Georges Lefebvre, *Napoleon: From Tilsit to Waterloo, 1807–1815.* Trans. J.E. Anderson. London: Routledge & Kegan Paul, 1969.

Ricardo Levene, *A History of Argentina.* Trans. and ed. William Spence Robertson. Chapel Hill: University of North Carolina Press, 1937.

Meriwether Lewis, *History of the Expedition.* New York: Allerton, 1922.

Martyn Lyons, *Napoleon Bonaparte and the Legacy of the French Revolution.* New York: St. Martin's Press, 1994.

Floyd J. Miller, *The Search for a Black Nationality: Black Emigration and Colonization, 1787–1863.* Urbana: University of Illinois Press, 1975.

Wilson Jeremiah Moses, ed., *Liberian Dreams: Back-to-Africa Narratives from the 1850s.* University Park: Pennsylvania State University Press, 1998.

Rory Muir, *Britain and the Defeat of Napoleon: 1807–1815.* New Haven, CT: Yale University Press, 1996.

Patrick O'Farrell, *England and Ireland Since 1800.* London: Oxford University Press, 1975.

Catherine Reef, *This Our Dark Country: The American Settlers of Liberia.* Boston: Clarion, 2002.

Donald H. Reiman, *Percy Bysshe Shelley.* Boston: Twayne, 1989.

William Spence Robertson, *Rise of the Spanish-American Republics as Told in the Lives of Their Liberators.* New York: D. Appleton, 1918.

Theodore Roosevelt, *The Naval History of the War of 1812.* New York: G.P. Putnam's Sons, 1900.

Alan Schom, *One Hundred Days: Napoleon's Road to Waterloo.* New York: Atheneum, Maxwell Macmillan International, 1992.

Percy Bysshe Shelley, *Shelley's Poetry and Prose.* 2nd ed. Ed. Donald H. Reiman and Neil Fraistat. New York: Norton, 2002.

Maynard Solomon, *Beethoven.* 2nd ed. New York: Schirmer, 1998.

J.C.A. Stagg, *Mr. Madison's War: Politics, Diplomacy, and Warfare in the Early American Republic.* Princeton, NJ: Princeton University Press, 1983.

Alexander Wheelock Thayer, *Thayer's Life of Beethoven.* Rev. and ed. Elliot Forbes. Princeton, NJ: Princeton University Press, 1967.

Harry E. Vanden, *Politics of Latin America: The Power Game.* New York: Oxford, 2002.

Jack Zipes, *Fairy Tale as Myth/Myth as Fairy Tale.* Lexington: University Press of Kentucky, 1994.

Web Sites

Discovering Lewis and Clark, www.lewis-clark.org. This Web site presents an impressive interactive multimedia history of the Lewis and Clark Expedition. New interpretive features are offered monthly.

Napoleonic Guide, www.napoleonguide.com. This expansive Web site contains a variety of historical information on Napoléon Bonaparte and the Napoleonic era. Numerous links are also provided.

Wikipedia: The Free Encyclopedia, http://en.wikipedia.org/wiki/Main_Page. This free online encyclopedia is a useful reference tool navigable by historical years, themed time lines, academic disciplines, and other classification schemes. It is available in a variety of languages.

INDEX